falling
into
Grace

Also by Adyashanti

Emptiness Dancing
True Meditation
The End of Your World

ADYASHANTI

falling into Grace

insights on the end of suffering

SOUNDS TRUE

Boulder, Colorado

Sounds True, Inc.
Boulder, CO 80306

© 2011, 2013 Adyashanti

SOUNDS TRUE is a registered trademark of Sounds True, Inc. All rights reserved. No part of this book may be reproduced in any manner without written permission from the author and publisher.

Published 2013

Cover and book design by Dean Olson

Printed in Canada

Library of Congress Cataloging-in-Publication Data
Adyashanti.
   Falling into grace : insights on the end of suffering Adyashanti.
      p. cm.
   ISBN 978-1-60407-087-3 (hardcover)
   1. Suffering. 2. Mind and body. 3. Peace of mind.
4. Suffering—Religious aspects. 5. Peace of mind—Religious aspects. I. Title.
   BF789.S8.A39 2011
   294.3'422—dc22

                                        2010035568

ISBN 978-1-60407-937-1
eBook ISBN 978-1-60407-332-4

10

Contents

Editor's Preface

IN THE SPRING of 2009, I was talking on the phone with Adyashanti about potential ideas for a new book and audio series with Sounds True. I mentioned that I wanted to publish a book of his teachings that would be welcoming to people who are new to the spiritual path, a book that would have reach as well as depth. Adya (as students and friends call him) surprised me and said, "The more I teach, the more I discover that the fundamentals are the most important part of any teaching. I notice that when I talk in a very clear way about essential spiritual insights, people who are newcomers as well as people who have been on the path for decades derive tremendous benefit."

This idea of a book on the "fundamentals of spiritual discovery" became the organizing principle for a series of talks given over five days in the fall of 2009, in Los Gatos, California. These talks were then transcribed and edited into *Falling into Grace*.

As you read *Falling into Grace*, my recommendation is that you take your time and attend as much as possible to what is evoked within you, to the moments of realization, to what Adya calls "ah-ha moments." In a sense, *Falling into Grace* is a transmission, a revealing of our true nature beyond any definition. Transmission is a heart-to-heart meeting in which we are directly shown, almost like the parting of a veil, certain truths about the boundlessness of being. The transmission occurs not at the level of the words, but at a feeling level, as part of a more subtle communication. The book is filled with pointers. The question is: Can we follow and fall into where the pointers lead?

Several years ago, I was interviewing Adya about his work, and I asked him what he thought about transmission. He said, "I don't talk about it much, but it is actually one of the most important aspects of my teaching." *Falling into Grace* is the opportunity for readers to meet Adya in this vast, open dimension of being, a meeting that frees our hearts and invites us to fall and fall and fall, without the need to land anywhere.

Tami Simon
Publisher, Sounds True

Introduction

I WAS REFLECTING recently on my many years of teaching. One of the things I've noticed is that the most transformative element of any spiritual teaching is its basics, its fundamentals. These are also the easiest to forget, because our minds have a natural tendency to move into complexity. The mind believes that the more subtle and complex something is, the more accurately it reflects reality. What I've seen, however, over the many years of my own teaching, is that it is actually the fundamentals of the teaching that are the most impactful; that it is the basic elements of the teaching that hold the true power to help transform our lives.

This observation has been one of the primary motivations for creating this book: to present the fundamental elements of my teaching, as I continue to see these as the most important aspects of my work. While there are more subtle and complex parts to the teaching, what I've seen is that these are actually not that important; time and time again, I've seen that the simpler the teaching is, the more powerful and transformative it is. Our minds have a hard time believing this—how something so simple can be so powerful. But I continue to see that by exploring the most basic elements of why we suffer and how we perceive life from the perspective of separation, that these are without a doubt the most transformative aspects of the teaching.

Beyond even any teaching, though, the aspect of spiritual life that is the most profound is the element of grace. Grace is something that comes to us when we somehow find ourselves completely available, when we become open-hearted and open-minded, and are willing to entertain the possibility that we may not know what we think we know. In this gap of not knowing, in the suspension of any conclusion, a whole other element of life and reality can rush in. This is what I call *grace*. It's that moment of "ah-ha!"— a moment of recognition when we realize something that previously we never could quite imagine.

Many circumstances and experiences are capable of opening us to this grace. Whether it's a beautiful moment in nature or spending time with someone we love or just sitting quietly in stillness, for some reason, a whole new perspective opens up. We find ourselves filled with grace. At other times, grace comes with a more fierce face. Somehow the difficult situations in our lives have a way of opening our hearts and minds the most. We do everything we can to avoid such moments, but in reality, it is these challenging moments that often offer the greatest opportunities for growth and the transformation of consciousness.

The teachings in this book are simply ways to open ourselves to grace, to open ourselves to that mysterious element of light that enters in the hidden and quiet moments. This sparks a revolution in the way that we perceive life, a revolution that goes a long way toward helping us to end the suffering and strife that so many human beings live with day to day.

The teachings in this book are not meant to be information for the mind to collect, but something to be deeply meditated on to see if you can find the truth in your own experience. You need to have the willingness to slow down, even stop, and fully digest what you hear, because ultimately, the truth of any teaching can never be found in the words. Rather, the truth is found in that which is revealed inside of our own selves. By exploring in this way, we make the teachings our own. And by making a teaching our own, by experiencing what the teaching is pointing to within our *own* experience, we come to awaken to a view of life that's more whole and unified—and, in the end, one that directly addresses the deepest yearning and longing of the human heart.

1

The Human
Dilemma

WHEN I WAS a young child, about seven or eight years old, one of the things I started to notice and ponder as I watched the adults around me was that the adult world is prone to suffering, pain, and conflict. Even though I grew up in a relatively healthy household with loving parents and two sisters, and actually had quite a wonderful and happy childhood, I still saw a great deal of pain around me. As I looked at the adult world, I wondered: How is it that people come into conflict?

As a child, I also happened to be a great listener—some may even say *an eavesdropper*. I would listen to every conversation that went on in the house. In fact, it was a family joke that nothing happened in the house without me knowing about it. I liked to know everything that was going on around me, and so I spent a lot of my childhood listening to the conversations of adults, in my home and the homes of relatives. Much of the time, I found what they talked about to be quite interesting, but I also noticed a certain ebb and flow to most of their discussions—how conversations moved into a little bit of conflict, and then sort of flowed back away from it, closer to conflict, then back away from it. Occasionally there would be an argument or hurt feelings, and people would feel misunderstood. It all felt very peculiar to me—and I really didn't understand why adults acted the way they did; the way they communicated and related with one another really baffled me. I didn't know exactly what it was that was happening, but something felt off.

BELIEVING WHAT WE THINK

As I watched and observed, day after day, week after week, month after month, even year after year, one day I had an epiphany: "Oh my gosh! Adults believe what they think! That's why they suffer! That's why they get into conflict. That's why they behave strangely, in ways that I don't understand, because they actually believe the thoughts in their head." Now, to a little child, this was actually quite a strange notion. It was a very foreign idea to me. Of course I had ideas in my head, but when I was a child, I didn't walk around like adults do, with a running, continuous commentary going on in my mind. Basically, I was too busy having fun, or listening, or being mesmerized or amazed by some aspect of life. What I realized was that adults spent a lot of time *thinking,* and more important than that—and more odd, it seemed to me—they actually believed what they were thinking. They believed the thoughts in their head.

All of a sudden, I had an understanding of what was happening when adults communicated with one another; that what people were in fact communicating were their thoughts, and that each person believed that what they thought was actually true. The problem was that all of the different adults had different ideas about what they thought the truth was, and so when they communicated there was this unspoken negotiation, this attempt to win each other over and to defend one's thinking and beliefs.

As I continued to observe how adults believed their thinking, it struck me, "They're insane! I understand them now: They're insane. It's insane to believe the thoughts in your head." In a strange way, to discover this as a child was quite a relief. It was a relief to at least begin to understand this strange world of adults, even though it didn't make much sense to me.

In sharing this experience over the years, I've learned that many others remember a similar insight when they were young, of the insanity of the adult world. Rather than providing a sense of relief, however, this insight causes many children to begin to question themselves, wondering if there is something wrong with them. It is a frightening experience for us as children to think that the adults we depend on for our survival, care, and love may actually be insane.

THE DILEMMA OF HUMAN SUFFERING

For me, for some reason that I don't really understand, this insight did not cause me to fear the adult world. Instead, it was actually a great relief that I could at least understand why they were doing what they were doing. Without knowing it, I was actually gaining my first insight into one of the great dilemmas of being a human being: the cause of human suffering. This is something the Buddha questioned over 2,500 years ago: What is the cause of suffering in the human being?

When any of us looks out into the world, of course we can see unimaginable beauty and mystery. There are many things to appreciate and be in awe of, but we can't really look out at the human world without acknowledging that there is also a great amount of suffering and discontent. There is a great amount of violence, hate, ignorance, and greed. Why is it that we human beings seem to be so prone to suffering? Why is it that we seem to hold onto it as if it was a very important possession?

Having grown up around dogs and cats, one of the things I noticed is that a dog could get upset with you—it could get resentful and disappointed; it could get its feelings hurt—but within minutes, or even sometimes seconds, the dog would just slough it off. It could put down its suffering and return back to its natural state of happiness in a very short period of time. I wondered, "Why is it that human beings have such a difficult time putting their suffering down? What's the reason that we often carry it around, when it becomes such a burden to us?" In some way, many people's lives are defined by the events that have caused them to suffer, and many are suffering over events that occurred long, long ago. These events are no longer happening, yet they are still being lived, in a sense, and the suffering is still being experienced. What is going on here?

This insight I had as a child, even though I didn't know how significant it was at the time, was the beginning of my understanding as to why it is that we suffer. It became very clear that one of the primary reasons we suffer is because we believe what we think, that the thoughts in our heads come uninvited into our consciousness, swirl around, and we attach to them. We identify with them and grab hold of them. This insight that I had as a child was much more significant than I realized. It took me many years, probably a good couple of decades, to realize that what I'd seen as a child struck at the root of why we actually suffer, that one of the greatest reasons that we suffer is because we believe the thoughts in our head.

Why is it that we do this? Why do we believe the thoughts in our head? We don't believe the thoughts in someone else's head, when they speak them to us. When we read a book—which is nothing but the recording of somebody else's thoughts—we can take them or leave them. But why is it that we are so prone to grasp at the thoughts that occur within our own mind—to hold onto them and become identified with them? We don't seem to be able to put them down even when they cause great pain and suffering.

THE SHADOW SIDE OF LANGUAGE

Much of our programming to believe our thoughts begins with our education and with the very natural process we all go through when we learn language. To a child, language is a great discovery. It's an amazing thing to be able to name something. It's highly advantageous to be able to point toward something and say, "That's what I want!" "I want a drink of water." "I want some food." "I want to have my diaper changed." It's a wonderful breakthrough when we first discover and begin to utilize language.

One of the most powerful pieces of language that we come upon when we're young is our own name, when we realize that we have a name. I remember this moment of realization in my own life. I used to just repeat my name over and over in my head, because it was so fun to do. It was a great discovery. "Oh! This is who I am!"

As we grow up, most of us have a certain infatuation with language. Language becomes quite useful in communicating amazing things, a powerful tool for sharing our experience and moving through life. As we age, it becomes a way for us to express great creativity and intelligence. But language also has a shadow side, as does everything. Thought, too, has a shadow side, and it's the shadow side of thought that we are uneducated about. Nobody tells us that to believe the thoughts in our minds might be a very dangerous thing to do. What we're taught is just the opposite. We're actually programmed as we grow up—by our parents, by the world around us, by each other—very much like a computer. We are taught to think in terms of absolutes. Something is either one way or the other, right or wrong, black or white. This programming thus affects the way we think and the way we perceive the world. Is it blue? Is it red? Is it big? Is it tall?

The great spiritual teacher Krishnamurti once said, "When you teach a child that a bird is named 'bird,' the child will never see the bird again." What they'll see is the word "bird." That's what they'll see and feel, and when they look up in the sky and see that strange, winged being take flight, they'll forget that what is actually there is a great mystery. They'll forget that they really don't know what it is. They'll forget that that thing flying through the sky is beyond all words, that it's an expression of the immensity of life. It's actually an extraordinary and wondrous thing that flies through the sky. But as soon as we name it, we think we know what it is. We see "bird," and we almost discount it. A "bird," "cat," "dog," "human," "cup," "chair," "house," "forest"—all of these things have been given names, and all of these things lose some of their natural aliveness once we name them. Of course we need to learn these names and form concepts around them, but if we start to believe that these names and all of the concepts we form around them are real, then we've begun the journey of becoming entranced by the world of ideas.

The capacity to think and utilize language has a shadow side that, if left unattended and used in an unwise way, can cause us to suffer and experience unnecessary conflict with one another. Because after all, that's what thought does: It separates. It classifies. It names. It divides. It explains. Again, thought and language have a very useful aspect and they are therefore very necessary things to develop. Evolution has worked very hard to make sure that we have the capacity to think coherently and rationally, or, in other words, to think in ways that will ensure our survival. But when we look back upon the world, we see that the very thing that has evolved to help us survive has also become a form of imprisonment for us. We've become trapped in a world of dreams, a world in which we live primarily in our minds.

This is the dream world that is addressed by many ancient spiritual teachings. When many of the old saints and sages say, "Your world is a dream. You're living in an illusion," they're referring to this world of the mind and the way we believe our thoughts about reality. When we see the world through our thoughts, we stop experiencing life as it really is and others as they really are. When I have a thought about you, that's something I've created. I've turned you into an idea. In a certain sense, if I have an idea about you that I believe, I've degraded you. I've made you into something very small. This is the way of human beings, this is what we do to each other.

To genuinely understand the cause of suffering and our potential release and freedom from it, we have to look very closely at this root of human suffering: When we believe what we think, when we take our thinking to be reality, we will suffer. It's not obvious until you look at it, but when we believe our thoughts, in that instant, we begin to live in the world of dreams, where the mind conceptualizes an entire world that doesn't actually exist anywhere but in the mind itself. At that moment, we begin to experience a sense of isolation, where we no longer feel connected to each other in a very rich and human way, but we find ourselves receding more and more into the world of our minds, into the world of our own creation.

COMING OUT OF THE MATRIX OF SUFFERING

So what's the way out? How do we avoid becoming lost in our own thoughts, projections, beliefs, and opinions? How do we begin to find our way out of this whole matrix of suffering?

To begin with, we have to make a simple, yet very powerful observation: All thoughts—good thoughts, bad thoughts, lovely thoughts, evil thoughts—occur *within* something. All thoughts arise and disappear into a vast space. If you watch your mind, you'll see that a thought simply occurs on its own—it arises without any intention on your part. In response to this, we're taught to grab and identify with them. But if we can, just for a moment, relinquish this anxious tendency to grab our thoughts, we begin to notice something very profound: that thoughts arise and play out, spontaneously and on their own, within a vast space; the noisy mind actually occurs within a very, very deep sense of quiet.

This may not be apparent on first observation, because we're used to thinking of silence and quiet in terms of the exterior environment: Is my home quiet? Has the neighbor's dog stopped barking? Is the TV turned off? Or we tend to think of quiet in internal terms: Is my mind noisy? Have my emotions calmed down? Do I feel settled? But the silence or quiet I'm talking about is not a relative silence. It's not an absence of noise, even of mental noise. Rather, it's about beginning to notice that there is a silence that is always present, and that noise happens within this silence— even the noise of the mind. You can start to see that every thought arises against the backdrop of absolute silence.

Thought arises literally within a thoughtless world—each idea appears in a vast space.

As we continue to look at the nature of thought, and in particular what or who it is that is aware of thought occurring, most of us are quite convinced, "Well, I'm the one that notices thought." This is what we've been taught and what we naturally assume—that "you" and "me," as separate individuals, are the ones who "think" our thoughts. Who else would be thinking them? But if you look closely, you'll realize that it's not actually true that *you* are the one thinking. Thinking simply happens. It happens whether you want it to or not, and it stops whether you want it to or not. As you start to see this process, it can be quite a shock that your mind just thinks on its own, and it stops on its own. If you stop trying to control your mind, you begin to notice that thought occurs in a very vast space. This is an extraordinary discovery, because it begins to show us that there is something present that is other than thought, and that we aren't just the next thought that we have in our minds.

When we believe in our thoughts, when we believe at the deepest level that they in fact are equal to reality, we can start to see how this leads directly to frustration, discontent, and ultimately to suffering on many levels. This realization is the first step in unraveling our suffering. There is something else, however, which needs to be seen—something even more fundamental. This deeper realization comes long after we've formed our opinions, our beliefs, and our capacity to conceptualize. Why is it that, even when we start to see that it is our minds that are making us suffer, we still grasp onto our minds so deeply and with such vehemence? Why do we still hold on to this identification, to such an extent that sometimes it feels like it's holding onto us? One of the reasons we do this is because we think that the content of our minds—our beliefs, our ideas, our opinions—are actually who we are. This is the prime illusion: that I am what I think, that I am what I believe, that I am my particular point of view. But to help us see through this illusion, it is helpful to look even deeper—into what it is that drives us to see the world in this way.

WHAT IS IT THAT WE'RE SEEKING?

There was a saying attributed to Jesus in *The Gospel of Thomas,* written shortly after Jesus's death, in which he says: "The seeker should not stop until he finds. When he does find, he will be disturbed. After being disturbed, he will be astonished. Then he will reign over everything." This was the first quote by Jesus in this gospel and, in many ways, it's the most shocking teaching in the whole collection of writings. "The seeker should not stop until he finds." What is the seeker seeking? What are you seeking? What are human beings really seeking? We all have many names for what we're seeking, but really, whether we call it God, whether we call it money, whether we call it approval, whether we call it power, whether we call it control, what we're really seeking is to be happy. We're only seeking these outward forms because we think if we attain them, we'll be happy. So really, no matter what we *say* we're seeking—God, money, power, prestige—what we're really seeking is happiness. If we didn't think that what we are seeking would give us happiness, we wouldn't seek it.

In this quote, Jesus begins with encouragement and direction by saying that the seeker should not stop until he finds—until he finds happiness, peace, or reality itself. And the truth is that until reality is seen clearly, as it is, there will be no lasting peace or happiness, so we must first find out what is real, who we are, and what life is at its core. We're encouraged to keep at it, going further and further, until we find. The challenge is that most of us have no idea how to seek. For most of us, seeking is just another form of grasping and attainment. But this isn't the kind of seeking that Jesus is referring to here.

Jesus is pointing to a way to seek that was revealed long, long ago: to seek within. If we really look at it, anything we can acquire from the outside will eventually fade away. This is the law of impermanence that the Buddha taught about thousands of years ago. Whether it is power, control, money, people, or health, everything that you see around you is in a process of arising and then decaying. Just as your lungs breathe in and then breathe out, it's necessary for things to fall away so that life can breathe new again. This is one of the laws of the universe: that everything you see, taste, touch, and feel will eventually disappear back into the source from which it came, only to be reborn and appear yet again, receding again back into the source.

In the second line of this saying, the power of this gospel is revealed: "When he does find, he will be disturbed." This line is pointing to why most people don't find lasting happiness—because most people don't want to be disturbed. Most of us don't want to be bothered. We don't want our search for happiness to have any difficulty in it. What we really want is to be given happiness on a platter. But to find what true happiness is, we must actually be willing to be disturbed, surprised, wrong in our assumptions—and cast into a very deep well of unknowing.

What does it mean to be disturbed, and why would we possibly open to this or desire it on any level? To understand this, we must look closely at our own minds, at those things we believe in, at the thoughts onto which we grasp. We must investigate our addiction to control, power, praise, and approval—all of the things that ultimately cause us to suffer. These things out in the world, which are external to us, may bring a certain temporary happiness and enjoyment, but they do not bring the deepest fulfillment for which we are all longing. They are incapable of addressing the question of why we suffer, and they are ultimately unable to bring the deepest relief to the human dilemma.

If someone said to you, "You can stop suffering. You can really stop suffering completely, right here and right now. All you have to do is to give up everything you think. You have to give up your opinions, you have to give up your beliefs, you have to even give up believing in your own name. You have to give all this up, but that's all you have to do. Give all of that up, and you can be happy, completely happy, free of suffering forever." For most people, this would be an unacceptable bargain.

"Give up my thoughts? Give up my opinions? If I did that, I'd be giving up who I am! No! I won't do that! I'd rather suffer than give up what I think, what I believe, what I'm holding on to. I'd rather suffer than give up my opinions!" This may sound ridiculous, but it's exactly the place that most people are in. This is the mind-state that most of us come from. When we're not willing to be disturbed, which means when we're not willing to find out that what we thought was real in fact wasn't real, we can never be happy. If we're not willing to find out that what we believe in really isn't the truth, then we can never be happy. If we're not honestly willing to look at the whole structure of who we think we are and be open to the idea that maybe we've been completely wrong about ourselves—maybe we're not who we thought we were at all—if we're not open to that idea, at least that possibility, there's no way we can find our way out of suffering.

This is why Jesus said that when you begin to find, you will be disturbed. When you begin to become conscious, more aware, when your eyes begin to open, the first thing you see is how deluded you are and how much you're holding onto that which makes you suffer. This is, in many ways, the most important step: Are you willing to be aware? Are you willing to open your eyes? Are you willing to be wrong? Are you willing to see that you may not be living from a standpoint of truth, from a standpoint of reality? This is what it means to be disturbed. But to be disturbed isn't a negative thing, not in the context in which I'm using the word here. To be disturbed means you're willing to see truth, you're willing to see that maybe things aren't the way you thought they were.

THE GREAT INTERNAL SPACE

What opens inside you when you're willing to entertain the possibility that things may be different than you thought they were is what I call the "great internal space": a place where you come to know that you don't know. This is really the entry point into the end of suffering: when you become conscious of the fact that you don't really know. I mean that you don't really know *anything*—that you don't really understand the world, you don't really understand each other, you don't really understand yourself. This is such an obvious thing when we really take a moment and look around. When we look at the world that human beings have created and how we relate to each other, it's so obvious that we don't really know anything at all. This is one of the things that I saw when I was a little child: This adult world has an insane quality to it. Everybody's going around pretending like they really know things, pretending like they know what's real and what's not, pretending they know what's right, pretending they know who's wrong, but actually nobody really knows. But this is something we're afraid of. We don't really want to admit that nobody really knows.

Again, we can see that there's a great unwillingness in most of us to be disturbed in this way. But if you've suffered enough—and I imagine that you have suffered plenty—then maybe you are willing to be disturbed. Maybe your suffering has created a longing for this great internal space.

Maybe you are willing to become open to the idea that you may be something completely different than you imagined yourself to be, that others may be completely different than you thought they were, that the world may be something completely different than you ever imagined. The place to start, as always, is with yourself. This is the entry point. Because, after all, this great internal space is within us. Our tendency, though, is to start with somebody else: "You change! You change, and then I'll be happy!" "If the world changes, then I'll be happy." "If my environment changes, or my work situation or my mate changes, then I'll be happy." But actually, we have to start with ourselves—not trying to "change" ourselves, because if we don't even know who we are, we won't know how to change ourselves. The first thing we have to look at is our own self, who we really are. Before we try to change anything about ourselves, we must first begin to know who and what we are, because by finding out what it is that we are, we step into a dimension of consciousness which brings an end to needless suffering.

So we begin to look into ourselves right now, in this very moment, wherever we are. I'm sitting here on a stool, and exactly where I am, when I look into what I am, I don't really know. I find that I'm an unfathomable mystery. I find that I could put a name onto myself, I could call myself any manner of names, I could come up with many descriptions for what I am, but really, all of these are just thoughts. When I look underneath the veil of thinking, what I find is that I am a mystery. In some ways, I disappear. I disappear as a thought. I disappear as an imagined someone. What I find, if I'm anything at all, is that I'm a point of awareness, recognizing that everything I think about myself isn't really what I am; I recognize that the next thought I have could never truly describe me.

What do you find when you look underneath the veil of your thoughts? What do you really find when you open up to something beyond your mind? What happens when you become still and you inquire, without just jumping at the next thought? Quietly ask, "What am I, really?" Isn't that moment absolute stillness? And aren't you completely aware of that stillness? And isn't it obvious that if we don't go to our minds, that what we are is something spacious and of amazing mystery, amazing wonder, that we are a still, quiet point of awareness and consciousness? Within this consciousness, within this space of stillness, many thoughts can and do appear. Many emotions can and do appear, many ways that we could imagine in our minds that we know. But really, it's all imagination. How do we know it's all imagination? Because when we stop imagining, it disappears. When we stop naming ourselves, who we think we are disappears until we begin to name ourselves again. But when we stop and we look, what's obvious is that there's just the looking, an open space of awareness, and nothing more, because the next thing is simply the next thought.

STANDING IN YOUR OWN AUTHORITY

Nobody told us that what we are is a point of awareness, or pure spirit. This isn't something we're taught. Rather, what we were taught was to identify with our name. We were taught to identify with our birth date. We were taught to identify with the next thought that we have. We were taught to identify with all the memories our mind collects about the past. But all that was just teaching; all that was just more thinking. When you stand in your own authority, based in your own direct experience, you meet that ultimate mystery that you are. Even though it may be at first unsettling to look into your own *no-thingness,* you do it anyway. Why? Because you no longer want to suffer. Because you're willing to be disturbed. You're willing to be amazed. You're willing to be surprised. You're willing to realize that maybe everything you've ever thought about yourself really isn't true.

When you're open to all that, then and only then can you stand in your own authority, on your own two feet. Only then can you really look for yourself underneath the mind and into the space between the next thoughts, to see clearly that what we are exists before we think about it. What you are exists before you name it. What you are exists before you even call it "male" or "female." What you are exists before we say "good" or "bad," "worthy" or "unworthy." What you are is more fundamental than what you say you are. What you really are is quite a surprise when you see it for the first time, when you feel it. You can start to feel your own transparency. You begin to recognize that it's possible that you really aren't a "someone" after all, even though the thoughts of a "someone" arise, even though in your life you often act as if you're someone. It's the way you get along in life. You respond to your name, you go to work, you do your job, you call yourself a husband or a wife or a sister or a brother. All of these are names we give to each other. All of these are labels. All of them are fine. There is nothing wrong with any one of them, until you actually believe they're true. As soon as you believe that a label you've put on yourself is true, you've limited something that is literally limitless, you've limited who you are into nothing more than a thought.

IMAGINING OURSELVES AND OTHERS

Let's look at how we form an image of ourselves out of nothing, because that's actually what we're doing. Out of this vast inner space of quiet and awareness, we form an image of ourselves, an idea of ourselves, a collection of thoughts about ourselves—this is something that we're taught to do when we're very young. We're given a name, we're given a gender. We acquire experience as we go through life, as we go through the ups and downs of what it is to be a human being; with each event that happens, the ideas we have about ourselves change. Bit by bit, we accumulate ideas of who we imagine ourselves to be. In a rather short time, by the time we're five or six years old, we have the rudimentary building blocks of a self-image. Image is something that, in our culture, we value very highly. We pamper our image, we clothe our image, we try to imagine ourselves to be more or better or sometimes even less than we really are. In short, we live in a culture in which the image we project to ourselves and to others is held as a very high value.

I remember when I was studying psychology in college and one of the topics was the importance of a good, healthy self-image. I was fascinated by the subject, and one day it occurred to me: "Image? Good image, bad image, it's just an *image!*" I realized that what we were being taught was to go from having a negative image of ourselves to a good image of ourselves. Of course, if we're going to stay in the realm of images, of believing that we're an idea or an image, then it's better to have a good image of ourselves than it is to have a negative image of ourselves. But if we're beginning to look at the core and the root of suffering, we start to see that an image is just that: It's an image. It's an idea. A set of thoughts. It's literally a product of imagination. It's who we imagine ourselves to be. We end up putting so much attention onto our image that we remain in a continuous state of protecting or improving our image in order to control how others see us.

So in effect, we are all walking around presenting an image to each other, and we're relating to each other as images. Whoever we think somebody else is, it's just an image we have in our mind. When we relate to each other from the standpoint of image, we're not relating to who each other is, we're just relating to our imagination of who each other is. Then we wonder why we don't relate so well, why we get into arguments, and why we misunderstand each other so deeply.

Everybody knows how painful it is and how much suffering it causes to walk around with a bad self-image. Almost all of us, either consciously or unconsciously, are in some process of trying to feel better about ourselves. It's very common that once you get through the façade of most human beings, what you find at the core is a feeling that the image they have of themselves is insufficient and not good enough. It's an image that seems in some way wounded—and it can never quite capture the essence of that person.

But there's something deeper going on here; there's a possibility of looking at image in a whole new way, from an entirely different vantage point. Allow yourself to see that your self-image is just an image—not reality, not the truth, not who we really are. We can think we're pretty good, or we can think we're really not so worthy, but either way, both of those conclusions are based on an image we have in our minds, which is something that we've inherited and created based on influences from our society, our culture, our friends, our parents, anyone with whom we've ever engaged. As we grow up, we gain the ability to re-create this self-image, but when we're young, society, parents, and culture condition us with an image of ourselves. When we transition out of childhood, we try to change our image—because we decide it doesn't fit, it doesn't feel quite right. It is like an old piece of clothing that we don't want to wear anymore. So we try something else on; we create new images, new illusions of who we imagine ourselves to be. But whatever this image is, when we look deep down in the core of all images, there is this feeling that we're faking it, this sense that we hope we don't get caught, because we're not really being who we are, that we really don't know who we are.

When I was quite young and I looked out at the world around me, I remember thinking, "Hey, everybody else seems to know who they are." Whether it was my friends or my parents, whether it was people whom I met as I went through life, I had this feeling that everybody seemed to know who they were, and they seemed to know what they were doing, with a fair amount of certainty. But as for myself, I felt like I was faking it. What I didn't realize was that everybody else was faking it, too! It looked like almost nobody else was faking it but me. But really, when I began to talk to more people about it, when I began to listen to what people said and how they said it, I began to realize that more people were faking being themselves than I had ever imagined.

THE DISCOVERY OF NO-IMAGE

If we're living from the standpoint of a self-image of who we think we are, who we imagine ourselves to be, this also creates an emotional environment. For example, if we think we're good and worthy, we'll create good and worthy emotions. But if we think we're unworthy, then we'll create negative emotions. So we can have a good or bad self-image, a self-image that feels emotionally either better or worse, but no matter what it is, if we look deeply at the core of all our images, there is this feeling of not being authentic, not being real. There's a reason for this. It's because as long as we're taking ourselves to be an image in our minds, we can't ever feel completely sufficient. We can't feel completely worthy. Even if the image is positive, we don't feel completely enlivened.

If we're willing to look in a deep way underneath the appearances, what we expect to discover—or perhaps hope to discover—is some great, shining image. Most people, deep in their unconscious, want to find an idea of themselves, an image of themselves, that's really good, quite wonderful, quite worthy of admiration and approval. Yet, when we start to peer underneath our image, we find something quite surprising—maybe even a bit disturbing at first. We begin to find no image. If you look right at this moment, underneath your idea of yourself, and you don't insert another idea or another image, but if you just look under however you define yourself and you see it's just an image, it's just an idea, and you peer underneath it, what you find is no image, no idea of yourself. Not a better image, not a worse image, but no image. Because this is so unexpected, most people will move away from it almost instinctively. They'll move right back into a more positive image. But if we really want to know who we are, if we want to get to the bottom of this particular way in which we suffer, arising from believing ourselves to be something we're not, then we have to be willing to look underneath the image, underneath the idea that we have of each other, and most specifically of ourselves.

What is the experience of feeling and knowing yourself as no image, no idea, no notion at all? At first, it might be disorienting or confusing. Your mind might think, "But there's got to be an image! I have to have a mask to wear. I've got to present myself as somebody or something, or in some particular way." But of course, that's just the mind, that's just conditioned thinking. It's really just the incarnation of fear, because there is a fear of knowing what we really are.

Because when we look into what we really are—underneath our ideas, underneath our images—there's nothing. There's no image at all.

There's a Zen *koan*—a riddle that you can't answer with your mind, but that you can only answer through looking directly for yourself—that says, "What was your true face before your parents were born?" So of course, if your parents weren't born yet, then you weren't born yet, and if you weren't born, then you didn't have a body, you didn't have a mind. So if you weren't born, you couldn't conceive of an image for yourself. It's a way, in a riddle, of asking: What are you, really, when you look beyond all images and all ideas about yourself, when you look absolutely directly, right here and right now, when you stand completely within yourself and look underneath the mind, underneath the ideas, underneath the images? Are you willing to enter that space, the place that casts no image, no idea? Are you really willing and ready to be that free and that open?

2

Unraveling
Our Suffering

HUMAN BEINGS HAVE always been compelled to reflect on their own lives, and one of the things that almost all human beings have noticed is that suffering is one of the most common components to being human. Throughout human history, many have tried to understand or explain suffering. All of our world religions are unique methods to address human suffering and the sense that so many feel of being alienated and cut off in some way. So many of us feel separate from one another, which further breeds a sense of fear and isolation. So there has always been this deep and abiding question, "Why is it that we suffer?"

It's not the only question that human beings have asked through the ages, but in some way it's the most intimate, because we're in fact biologically hardwired not to suffer. In other words, when we feel conflict, when we feel some sort of anxiety, our bodies get tense. When we suffer, our bodies respond directly—our breathing changes, our heart rate changes; our bodies send signals that something's not quite right. In many ways, we're biologically impelled to find a way not to suffer. So strangely, even though we seem biologically designed not to suffer, we still do.

It's as if we're actually wired to be happy; when we feel happy, even our bodies operate at their optimum level. When we feel good, we are open and we tend to be healthier and more energetic. Everything about our being, about this entire mechanism that evolution has created, seems to be hooked up to be happy, to be at peace, to be loving, and to be open. And yet one of the most common experiences human beings have, at a very deep place inside that we often try to hide or deny, is this ongoing element of human suffering.

So let us look even more deeply at the whole notion of suffering, of why we suffer, and explore whether there is a way to get out of suffering in any given moment, not necessarily getting out of future suffering, because the future will always remain something that's unknown.

When we begin to look at the cause of suffering, it reveals itself to be very simple. We often think that the source of the hurt lies somewhere outside of ourselves—that it's raining today, or it's too windy and we're cold, or someone said something that was harmful to us, or a family member treated us harshly when we were young, and on and on and on go all of the various reasons that we think we suffer. But where is the place from which suffering arises? Is there an essential point from which suffering ensues? When we really begin to look at suffering, what suffers is me and you. It's our sense of self that suffers, that feels strain, anxiety, alienation, and loneliness. Of course, it's the same self that feels happiness, joy, love, and peace, but what is it about this "self" that makes it so prone to suffering?

On closer examination, we see that one of the predominant qualities of self-consciousness is that we feel separate, that we feel "different than." I am a self here, and you are a self there. It's something that naturally and spontaneously comes upon us at birth. When we're born, we begin the process of becoming individuated, or, in other words, separate. If you've ever watched an infant, they can stare at themselves in the mirror for quite some time, fascinated. When they're very young, they'll stare at themselves in this way with no recognition. But as the months go on, even before they have language, you can see the moment when infants start to recognize that what they're seeing in the mirror is themselves. Then they get quite interested, quite fascinated as they look at this bundle of mystery in the mirror and have some rudimentary recognition that "that's me!"

As life goes on, the child will learn his or her name and a whole host of human values, mores, and systems of thought: what's right, what's wrong, what should be, what shouldn't be, who should have done what, who shouldn't have done what, and so on. As I mentioned earlier, as we grow up, we learn this whole conceptual world, this whole way of thinking. We're brought up and initiated into the way that human beings think—the way they conceptualize life, the way they look at life—and bit by bit, as we grow up, we take on our culture's way of seeing life, of seeing ourselves, seeing each other, and also seeing the world at large. In terms of how suffering originates, we can start to see that it originates with the creation of a "you" and a "me"—with this separate sense of self.

OPENING THE DOORWAY TO SUFFERING

What is it about a sense of self that gives rise to suffering? When there's no sense of self, we can still feel pain, and we can feel even a certain type of anguish. An infant can be angry, it can cry, it can scream, but this is essentially a different type of suffering than we encounter when we become adults, conscious of who we are. There's something about the perception of being a self, a someone, a something different and independent from everything else, that gives rise to suffering. As we grow older, we start to develop what's called an ego. Our ego is, in its most generic sense, our sense of who we are. An egoic sense of who we are means we essentially see ourselves as separate, as other from the world around us.

Initially, this sense of otherness isn't really a problem. In fact, as we've seen, it's actually a great discovery when children begin to discover their otherness. It's when they start to say, "This is mine, not yours. That's mine! Gimme this! I want this! I want that!" that things begin to shift. At the beginning, learning this way of seeing the world feels quite empowering to children. That's why they use it so much. When they discover their rudimentary sense of self, it helps them find a certain equilibrium in the world. It helps them locate "Here I am, as opposed to you." This seems to be something that's necessary. I say it *seems* to be necessary, because it happens for almost every human being. Every human being will develop a sense of a separate self, an ego structure. So it wouldn't really make any sense to say that it's wrong or that it shouldn't happen, because it does happen, and it happens almost all the time, for almost all human beings.

But there's a shadow side to our sense of self: When we see ourself as separate, as something other than the life around us, it breeds a sense of alienation and a sense of fear. Because when we see life as other, when we see each other as "other," then these "others" are seen as potential threats. Of course, life itself is one of the biggest threats that an ego can perceive. Life is an immense happening. You can go on a trip, you can go on vacation, you can go to the other side of the earth, but still you can't escape life. You can go to the moon, but still you can't escape life. You can't escape existence. As long as we see existence as something that's essentially other than what we are, we'll view existence as a potential threat. Seeing existence as a potential threat breeds fear, which in turn breeds conflict and suffering. When we see ourselves as essentially separate, then we start to think that I have to take care of "me," that *my* needs and *my* wants are of utmost importance, and so we have to make sure that we get what we want, irrespective of what someone else may want or need. So one of the first deep insights that can come to you is that all suffering is based on a misperception of self. As soon as we conclude that we exist as a separate self, then we've opened the doorway to suffering.

To be clear, I'm not suggesting that anyone should try to get rid of their sense of self. Everyone needs a sense of self. Just imagine if you had no sense of self whatsoever. If you were hungry, you literally wouldn't know where to put the food. Do you put it in your mouth, or do you put it in a mouth over there? Which mouth does it go in? If you had no sense of self, you literally wouldn't know how to operate in the world. If you were thirsty, you wouldn't know where to put the water. It seems quite strange, but it's actually possible to get into very, very deep meditative states where all sense of self is obliterated, where the self disappears temporarily. The problem with this is you become completely nonfunctional. You really can't do anything at all. So to have a sense of self, a feeling of "Here I am!" is very important. In fact, it's biologically hardwired into our system.

But that's where the potential misperception begins, because when we're given a name, we intuitively put it right onto that sense of self, and now our sense of self has a name; and then it has an age, and as life goes on, it has a thing called *a history.* The older we get, the more dense the sense of a separate self gets. Our sense of self becomes more and more contracted, and more and more solidifed and, in a sense, real. And the more real it feels, the more we feel that it needs to be protected, that it needs to get its way. The more real our sense of separateness feels, the more we'll feel an equal desire to control our environment and to control others so that we make sure we get what we want.

Often I am asked the question, "How can there be a *sense* of self without there being a self in actuality?" The example

I like to use to explore this is that the sense of self is like a perfume. It's a feeling that you have in your being that permeates who and what you are. As I've said, it helps orient you to the world, and it helps you function. It's like a perfume in the sense that when you feel into the sense of self, what you find is that it's more of a feeling than a thing. In that sense, it's like a scent that is distributed throughout your entire being. There's just a sense of it being here, a sense of its "existencing."

The mind then starts adding onto this rudimentary sense of self. The first thing it adds on is a thought, and it's called "I" or "me." Even with that first thought, you can feel the sense of self becoming more dense, more contracted, more stable—no longer so flowy or perfume-like. Rather, it starts to take on the quality of something that has its own place, something that is different than the world around it. And on and on the mind will go, creating a more and more elaborate self, and it will use this sense of self as proof that there must actually be a self.

EGO IS NOTHING BUT A STATE OF CONSCIOUSNESS

All of the great spiritual teachings direct us to look within, to "know thyself." Unless we know ourselves, we can never find our way beyond suffering. In fact, it's because we don't know ourselves that we're so prone to suffering, that we're so prone to misunderstanding the nature of who we are and reality itself. So this assumption that we are something separate, something other than everything around us, is the basis of what I call our "egoic consciousness." Because, after all, what we are really talking about here is a state of consciousness, a way of packaging the world conceptually. When our mind starts to imagine that we are something separate and different from the world around us, it changes the way we perceive, which means it changes our state of consciousness. The thoughts that we believe alter and change our state of consciousness.

You can see this shift in consciousness in any given moment, as you become aware of the thoughts that are present. Take the following thoughts, for example: imagine a sunny day on the beach, where you're lying in complete relaxation and you can hear the water lapping up against the shore. You can feel the warm sand supporting you from underneath. You can feel the rays of the sun across your face. You can hear the distant bird calls of seagulls. If you just think those thoughts, and allow yourself to really feel them, they'll start to change your consciousness. You'll literally start to feel different about this moment, even though nothing has actually changed, even though you're not actually at the beach. Even though all of it is created in your mind through imagination, it can change the way you feel, and how you feel affects how you perceive yourself, others, and the world around you.

So to take it a step further, when our mind interprets our sense of self to mean that there actually *is* self, our consciousness changes. And before very long, our consciousness is such that everywhere it looks, it sees separation. Of course, it doesn't tell you this. Most human beings don't walk around saying to themselves, "I feel separate from everything around me. I'm distinct and different." That's because this change of consciousness, this egoic consciousness, becomes so integrated into the way you see and experience life that you don't even have to remind yourself of it. You don't even have to be consciously thinking about it because it is so deeply woven into the fabric of your perception. The truth is that, ultimately speaking, ego is nothing but a state of consciousness.

If this was fully understood in its deepest aspect, that the ego is just a state of consciousness, we wouldn't be chained to it. We wouldn't be weighed down by it. We wouldn't feel isolated. Yet we see our egos, we see ourselves, as very separate entities; and everyone around us is doing the same thing. Everyone around us sees themselves as essentially different from others, and from life in general. So we move in a world where almost everyone we meet will be reflecting back to us this egoic sense of consciousness. To find liberation, we must wake up from this dream that our mind creates, that we're something separate than everything around us. This is the only way we can begin to find a way out of suffering.

In actuality, the ego is a fiction. It's really nothing more than a story in the mind. For some people, this idea is revolutionary. Some may even think to debunk the idea of ego is dangerous, silly, or ridiculous. How could my whole sense of myself, my whole sense of being an individual, be a fiction? How could this sense of self merely be something that I created in my mind?

THE DISAPPEARANCE OF THE PAST

I'd like to share with you a short exercise that will help illustrate what I'm saying. Just for a moment—let's say five seconds—and in these five seconds, let yourself stop thinking about anything—about yourself, about others, about the day. Just for five seconds, let your mind become quiet. What is it that actually happens in these five seconds? Maybe you think that the only thing you experienced was a quiet mind. But if you begin to really examine what happens when you're not thinking about yourself, you might see that you are no longer separate anymore, you aren't "other"; and in these moments, you will notice that your whole past disappears. This may be frightening for some, to see that when you're not thinking about your past, that it's literally not there.

Isn't this actually quite obvious, though? Whatever happened even one second ago isn't happening now, and it never will happen again. Whatever happened one minute ago, or a week ago or a month ago, ended almost as fast as it happened. But of course, we recorded it in our mind. Our minds are akin to a tape-recording device in that they record the past and then replay it in the present. But what the mind is replaying is a mental representation of the past, not the actual past itself. When you stop thinking, all there is is now. You have to conjure up an idea of yesterday for it to exist, and when we remember yesterday, when we remember a moment in the past, we actually think that it really exists. Worse than that, we believe that we remember the past accurately! But every study that's been done examining memory and how accurately we remember past events shows us that our minds begin to distort the past almost immediately.

In a well-known study conducted to measure memory retention, a group of college students were told a very short, thirty-second story. The researchers said, "We're going to tell you this story, and all we want you to do is remember it as accurately as you possibly can. Then we're going to have you tell it back to us at various intervals." And so the students would listen to the story, knowing that their only task was to remember it as accurately as possible, and then, one minute later, they would be asked to repeat the story. Five minutes later, they'd be asked to repeat it again; and then a half an hour later, and then an hour later, and then twelve hours later, and then a day later, and then two days later, and then a week later, and then finally, two weeks later.

What the researchers found was that, in the very first retelling of the story, after only one minute, the students were actually already beginning to distort it, that their memories weren't as accurate as they imagined. Even though the researchers were telling the story to very intelligent college students, with the relatively easy task of simply remembering the story, what they found was that when the students started to retell the story, within the third or fourth retelling, it became so different that it began to appear almost unrecognizable in relation to the original tale. And that was just within the third or fourth retelling, within an hour or two of having heard it. By a week later and certainly by two weeks later, the story was so distorted that you almost couldn't imagine that the retelling ever came from the original story. And yet all of the students truly believed that they were remembering the story quite accurately.

It has been demonstrated again and again that our memories of the past aren't actually memories, but rather re-creations and re-framings of thoughts and images. It comes as a surprise to many of us how inaccurate our recollections actually are. Most of us feel strongly that what we remember about a past event is actually how it occurred; we do not believe that we might have a "selective" memory. We think, "Oh, I definitely remember what happened. It's still so vivid in my mind!"

The truth that is being revealed here is that once a moment is gone, it is actually gone. And when you're not thinking yourself into existence, there really isn't a self. All you have to do is try it for a moment. Just be still for five seconds. What happens to your name, your gender, and the person you imagine yourself to be?

If we're to find a way beyond suffering, we're going to have to look at this sense of self that's really nothing but a collection of memories projected into the present moment and then into the future. We're going to have to begin to notice that what we think we are is just that: simply a thought. What we imagine ourselves to be, it's just that. It's imagination. Neither our thoughts nor our imagination can tell us who we are.

It's quite astonishing to open completely to the idea that you're not what you think you are, that you're not the story of you in your mind. This is revolutionary if you really begin to see it for yourself. It begins to call into question the very essence of who and what you are, and by looking at yourself in this way—by looking at how your mind creates your sense and image of self—you begin to feel some distance from your mind. After all, what is it that's noticing your thoughts about yourself? What is it that's seeing the mind, recognizing it? What is it that notices all of the ideas that you have about yourself? What is it that looks at the self-image? What is it that feels this sense of being a separate self? Just by living with questions like these, space opens within your mind, and you begin to realize that maybe you're not really your mind, that maybe your mind is just something that happens within you, that thoughts are something that just occur on their own, without the next step of then implying that there is a "thinker" who is thinking them. The question then becomes: What is it that these thoughts are occurring within? Who or what is aware of them?

THREE WAYS OF SUFFERING
The Illusion of Control

We'll take some time to explore these questions later in this book, but for now, we're going to explore three common ways that our egos cause us to suffer—beyond the most basic observation that it is our thoughts that bring about our suffering. The first way is probably the deepest rooted of them all: our desire to control. As soon as we imagine ourselves to be somebody separate from everyone else, from the life that we see all around us, we'll naturally have an inner sense that life is something we need to control. In order to stay safe, secure, and separate, we need to control not only ourselves but others, and the circumstances all around us. However, because the truth is that we do not have *any* control, we inevitably find ourselves in quite a bind.

The reality is that we don't have any control; the ego has no control over how reality unfolds and reveals itself. How is it the case that the ego doesn't have control? Simply because ego is merely a thought in your mind. It's an image. It's a way your mind references itself, thinks about itself, and creates a sense of self in the first place. If your whole egoic self is merely a product of imagination, a mechanical result of thoughts linking themselves together, then it's obvious that a thought doesn't have any control. A thought is just something that occurs. It happens and then passes away.

This is a very challenging and at times frightening thing to see, especially if we believe that we are our egos. Life, however, shows us continuously, over and over, that we really don't have the control that we want or think we have. Just look inside your own mind. You don't really have control whether one thought enters or exits your mind. If you don't even have control of the thoughts that appear in your head, how much control do you really have? If you really have control, wouldn't you just decide to feel good all the time—open, loving, and happy? And isn't it odd that even though life shows us over and over again that the ego doesn't have control, we keep believing that it does? We keep insisting that it does, because if it doesn't, that would be too overwhelming! It would seem like the worst thing that an ego could ever realize is that it doesn't have control, because if an ego doesn't have control, then it really has no hope. It has no way out. It has no way to make life into what it wants it to be.

It would be a terrible thing, indeed, if we actually were our egos, if we actually were the thought-created self in our mind. But we're not. Rather, what we really are is that which watches the mind, what notices the mind, and what is aware of all mental activity, including the desire to control. If you genuinely begin to look at the whole notion of control, it really begins to open up the mind. And that's what's necessary if we want to end our persistent suffering: we have to open up the way we think. Eventually, we may open up right beyond thought itself. But initially, we have to open up what we're willing to think about and the conclusions we're willing to come to. When we're in our egos, we'll naturally try to control each other, as well as ourselves. We're trying to control life. But I'm sure you've noticed that you can't control life. The sun comes up when it wants, and it sets when it wants, not when you or I want it to set. The rain comes whether you want it to or not, and the moon rises whether you want it to or not, just like it sets. And the same is true with each moment, and with everyone we meet. We think we're in control, but it's an illusion. It's a deception.

This deception is created in our minds, and in some ways it's the most convincing deception there is, because as long as we think we're in control, as long as we think we *can* control, then we'll stay chained to the state of egoic consciousness. On the surface, the illusion of control makes us feel safe and able to create a life for ourselves of comfort and security, manipulating our lives based on what we think we need. Yet, in actuality, we have no such control. Still, the illusion of it is amazing in its design and its complexity, because after all, almost every human being falls for it. Almost every human being thinks, "I'm in control of my life," except when times get really difficult.

There are times when you're almost forced to recognize that you aren't in control. A painful emotion arises, and you can't run away from it. You can't make it vanish. All of a sudden, it's obvious: "I'm not in control!" which often causes a deeper panic. "Oh no! I'm not in control! I can't change this feeling! What do I do? How do I change this?" Isn't it ironic that even though we see that we have no control, we still habitually grab onto it? Isn't that the definition of insanity: to keep trying to do the same thing, expecting different results? But literally, we can spend a whole lifetime trying to exercise this sense of control that we don't really have.

Demanding That Things Be Different

Another way that our minds create suffering is through the demands we make on life and on others. In one sense, ego is a demanding machine: "I want this!" "I want that!" "I don't want this!" "I don't want that!" "You should be like this!" "You shouldn't have done that to me!" "I shouldn't feel the way I feel!" All demands, at their essence, are ways that we try to manipulate reality, ways that we insist that life be different than what it is. It's not always obvious the degree to which we approach life in this way. If we look closely, however, we can see how pervasive this tendency is; in any given moment you are likely to be making unconscious, subtle demands upon life to be different.

We look to everything in life to make us happy, not realizing that happiness is actually at our very core. It's natural to our being. There's no way to *become* happy. We simply need to stop doing the things that make us unhappy. One of the ways that we make ourselves tremendously unhappy is through making demands of ourselves and each other. It's very common in human interaction for us to demand that someone change so that we can be happy, or fulfilled. In this process, we completely disregard what might be in the best interest of the other person, or in the interest of the whole. Is this really an expression of love? Is this ultimately what we want? Do we really want everyone around us to be changing to make us happy? Do we really want to be that kind of a tyrant? Does that really speak to our deepest heart, to the love that we all have inside?

When we insist that the things, people, and events around us change so that we can be happy, we're actually denying something very deep within us. We're denying the truth of who we are. We're denying the truth of each other. We're imagining that happiness depends on the events and circumstances of our lives—and on the people in our lives. We believe that if everyone in our life could be "just so," then we'll be content.

So this desire for demands—just like the desire for control—actually arises out of this state of consciousness called the egoic state of consciousness, where we imagine ourselves, and everyone else, to be different and separate. But again, the notion that we are separate is not really true; it's all made up. It's all conjured up in our mind. It's one big dream that we have. The difficulty with this dream is that almost everybody around us is having the same dream. It's essentially the collective dream of humanity. So it's not just you or me that's dreaming; almost all human beings are also having this dream of being separate, of being completely other than the world around them. What this means is that we really have to look within ourselves quite deeply, because we're not only looking beyond our own deluded mind, our own misunderstanding; we're looking beyond the delusion of the entirety of humanity.

Arguing with What Is

Another thing we do when we feel separate is that we argue with what is and what was. This is the third most common way that we suffer. In fact, if you want to guarantee your suffering, argue with what is. People often ask me, "What do you mean by 'what is'?" "What is" is this moment—before you even think about it. That's what is. Argue with this moment, and you will suffer. There's no way to argue with this moment and not suffer. That goes for the past, as well. Argue with the past, decide what has been shouldn't have been, and you'll suffer.

I realize that this may sound overly simplified, and it even sounds almost insulting. Most human beings, after all, feel justified in thinking that what was in the past shouldn't have been. We've all had difficult moments. We've all had moments when we've been hurt, maybe even abused. We've all had moments when people have treated us unkindly or destructively. It's natural to look back on those moments and think in our minds, "That moment shouldn't have been!" "So and so should not have behaved that way!" That thought, that conclusion, seems so justified. Because everybody around us would agree with it, we don't even question it. In fact, it might seem crazy or offensive to accept what has been. But what has happened in the past is neither good nor bad. It just is what was. So, when we argue with what was and we say, "It shouldn't have happened," we suffer. It's that simple.

I'm in no way suggesting that we deny what was. I'm not saying that you have to pretend like something in the past didn't hurt, didn't confuse you, or didn't cause you great pain. What I'm saying is, when you argue with it, when you say that something that happened shouldn't have happened, you suffer. Whatever happened is what happened. Whether it was good or terrible, it is what happened. Whatever's happening *now* is what's happening. We don't have to call it "good" or "bad." It may be painful; it may not be painful. We may like it; we may not like it. Whatever's happening this moment is what's happening. When you argue with it, when you say that what is happening shouldn't be happening, you suffer.

Refraining from arguing with the present moment—or the past—may at times feel dangerous. We might even feel fear: "If I don't argue with what's happening now, maybe it will never change." Because if our hearts and minds are open, we can't help but see a tremendous amount of suffering, pain, and conflict in the world. In the face of this, the truth of this, it may almost seem like an insult to not declare, "This shouldn't happen!"

But as soon as we say something shouldn't be happening, we've locked ourselves into an extremely narrow mindset with very few options. When we really see that what is, simply is—neither good, nor bad—then all options are available to us. We can then respond to life in a wise and loving way. It doesn't mean we just say to ourselves, "What is, is," and we do nothing. When we see and stay with what is, it actually opens up creative responses, new ways of seeing and engaging with "what is," which aren't based on separation or denial or trying to control, but instead are sourced in the human heart—in love, compassion, and wisdom.

This is also true for the past. When we let go of believing that some part of our past shouldn't have been, when we finally begin to let go of that—without pretending that the painful moments didn't happen—then we're open to a creative relationship with the past. We are able to fully embrace everything that ever was, even if it was terribly painful. Because after all, everything helped us get to this moment, right now. And this moment, right now, is the only moment where we have the capacity to wake up, to put an end to suffering, and that makes this moment worth all of the other moments that ever happened. This is the moment that we can end suffering. This is the moment when we can wake up from all of our stories of the past, present, and future.

* * *

In order to wake up, we must learn how these three tendencies—trying to control, making demands, and rejecting "what is"—fuel the suffering in our lives. We have to somehow find the capacity to really want to know what's true, in this moment, without trying to control or make demands of it, because it's the truth that delivers us from suffering. It's the truth that allows us to shift out of this egoic state of consciousness that we seem so trapped in, into a whole different state of consciousness, which is much more open, free, and inclusive—and infinitely more creative. In the ego, our options are very limited, and they've all been tried before; all of the solutions the ego has come up with have failed. If you wonder if they've failed, just turn on the television. Read the newspaper. There are still wars. There is still cruelty. There are still human beings all over the place not being open, loving, and available to one another. Clearly, something different is needed. As we've seen, to do the same thing over and over, expecting different results, is literally a form of insanity. And this is, in many ways, the world that we live in.

THE STICKY NATURE OF GENERATIONAL SUFFERING

Now I want to introduce a different type of suffering, one that can be particularly difficult to unravel. Over my years of teaching, I've noticed that there's a particular type of suffering that is sticky, pervasive, and often very hard to find your way out of. I've come to call this "generational suffering." The notion of generational suffering is based on the fact that each of us comes from a generational line, which goes as far back in time as we can imagine, back even to the original human beings, our original ancestors themselves. We're actually the outcome of a long chain of many,

many generations. Each of our family systems is imbued with a tremendous amount of beauty and goodness, and also carried within these systems, as we all know, is what we might call "generational pain," or "generational suffering." This is an actual energy that is unconsciously passed down from one generation to the next.

If you look closely at a particular family system, you'll see the pain that tends to be passed down through a family lineage. For example, parents who have a particular tendency to suffer with anger or depression tend to produce children who suffer from the same afflictions, and then these children produce children who suffer with the same, and so on. Generational suffering is very insidious. It becomes deeper and deeper ingrained in a family as time wears on, and it forms the core of much of the suffering that people experience.

One of the interesting things to note about generational suffering is that it's not personal. In other words, it's more like a virus that infects the people within a family. It's a way of suffering that infects a family and then gets passed on, almost like the flu or a cold, through future generations. When you're born, without even knowing it, you're actually being handed this generational pain. In response, you will complain about it, think it's terrible, or otherwise resist it. But by doing so, you will come to see that denial or complaints about this pain only makes it sink more deeply into your being.

When you start to identify how this generational suffering operates in your life, when you see how your particular way of suffering is similar to the way others in your family suffer, it can open your heart and mind. From this wider perspective, you can actually start to let go of blame and see that those who passed down suffering to you through this generational chain were themselves experiencing the pain and quite unconscious of what was happening. This pain just came to them, and they manifested it in whatever way they did, and then they unknowingly passed it down to the next generation.

Some of the deepest pain and wounding that we carry with us throughout our lives comes via this generational suffering. I often ask people, when they identify a difficult feeling such as anger, upset, rage, or resentment: "Which of your parents does this feeling remind you of: your mother or your father?" Usually, when they touch upon some of their deepest emotional woundings, they'll immediately be able to tell me which parent it came from. When you're able to see this clearly, you see that your mother or your father, or your uncle or aunt, in fact had the same wounding that you did. They passed it on to you by acting it out, in the same way their parents passed it on to them.

Eventually, this energy comes to you, and you become the forefront of this generational pain. It's easy to get resentful and blame this pain on someone else, but when you really see the nature of it, you see that it's not personal, even though the implications for you feel very personal, and maybe the way it was acted out was also very personal. But the pain itself, the suffering itself, is really not *you*. It was handed down unconsciously from one person to the next, from one generation to the next. Of course the way it gets handed down is often extraordinarily painful, sometimes violent, because it seems that you are the target of this suffering as it manifests in you and in the family members around you. But if you can avoid getting completely lost in the anger or the resentment—even though, from a relative perspective, it's understandable—if you can withhold your judgment for just a moment, you will start to see that the pain that you feel was in large part suffering from others in your family—and it does not have to be your own.

When you feel and can identify this deep pain within you, see that blaming others in your family is not the solution. When you feel the urge to blame, keep in mind that your generational line has lived with the same pain, too. It is highly likely that they never even imagined that it was generational. They probably took it very personally, and therefore their only option was to act it out. When you start to see this in terms of a long chain of suffering handed down from generation to generation, and you realize that you're the one, here and now, who can become conscious of how this works, then you have the opportunity to put an end to it.

The process of unraveling this suffering won't necessarily be easy, fun, or enjoyable, but it does mean you can radically change your perspective on it. Whenever we become conscious or more aware of something that's painful, it is often the case that the pain may be heightened for a while. It's as if we're starting to come out of a certain emotional numbness, and we may find ourselves resenting and blaming others as we start to relate directly with the suffering. But the more we look outward, resenting and blaming others and particular life circumstances, the more unconscious we become, and the more the pain and suffering is sent deeper into our systems. And the more deeply it is buried within us, the more it gets transferred to those we love—our children, friends, family members, and so on. Although it can be quite painful, we can come to see that we have a precious opportunity, through our own awareness and direct seeing, to finally allow it to end.

* * *

Even though pain and suffering can be generational, as we're seeing, it can only be maintained in the present within the structures of our own mind—by believing our own thoughts of separation, blame, and condemnation. Coming to the end of suffering is really about beginning to see all of the ways that our mind maintains suffering through habitual patterns of thinking. As we begin to understand the causes of suffering, that all of our suffering is based in various ways in which we imagine ourselves to be separate and different, we begin the process of waking up, from unhappiness to happiness. We also begin to realize that, even though we've had suffering handed down to us through our family lines, even though we've lived our entire lives with these mental constructs that lead to our pain, we are actually quite fortunate, as we have the capacity to put an end to the suffering now, simply by becoming aware of it.

The direct confrontation with suffering can and often is quite painful when we first begin to look at it. It's like when you have a limb that's numb because the blood hasn't flowed in it, and when the blood starts to flow, it hurts for a while. You have that sort of "pins and needles" feeling as the blood comes back into the veins and life comes back into the limb. That's part of waking up, part of coming out of the dream of the mind. But it's essential that we do so, and it's essential that we allow ourselves to go through this process of un-numbing ourselves, coming out of the imagination of our minds—not just for ourselves, but also so we can cease bringing suffering to others because of our unconscious behaviors. Then we become part of the answer to humanity's suffering. As long as we're asleep within our egos, we aren't really contributing either to ourselves or to anyone else. As we begin to awaken from this egoic state of consciousness, we begin to suffer less and less, and as we suffer less, we cause less suffering in the world around us. It's a gift we give to the world, and it's a gift that the world is happy to receive. Just like we wish to be happy and free from suffering, so do all living beings. We all have the opportunity to end suffering in our own lives, and to help all others do the same.

3

Awakening from the Egoic Trance

IF WE REALLY want to address the whole issue of suffering, as well as our desire and yearning for freedom, love, and connection, then we need to learn how to look clearly at our own minds. As we've seen, when we begin to look into the nature of the mind—and at the thinking process itself—we see how thinking creates this sense of separation and isolation. Through careful inquiry, we discover that the process of identification, the root of our suffering, begins with the rudimentary structure of thought itself. Thought is symbolic. A thought isn't a thing. It has no reality; it is only an abstraction. A thought is, at best, a description of something we take in with our senses. And yet, from a very young age, we're taught that we *are* what we think about ourselves. But there is another layer to this, and that is we tend to believe that we are what others think about us. We derive our view of ourselves from our parents, our friends, our community, our teachers, our sisters, our brothers, from everybody who gives us feedback about ourselves.

The difficulty of this and the problem with it is that the images we have of ourselves are often in conflict—because the perceptions and thoughts that others have about us don't always "agree" with one another. At one moment, we have an image of ourself as being a worthy, loving, and happy person—but within minutes or an hour, our image of ourself can change quite drastically. All of a sudden, we may decide that we're a terrible person because someone was critical of us, said something unkind about us, or told us that they really didn't like us anymore. The idea we have of ourselves is something that makes us feel very insecure, because it can change so quickly, and often at the hands of another. And so we suffer, because someone's opinion of us can so easily trigger anger, sadness, even depression. Our sense of self is very ephemeral; it's not as solid as we imagine it to be, and the confusion around it is one of the greatest causes of human suffering that there is. To address the dilemma of human suffering, we need to look even more closely at the way our minds create this shifting sense of who we are.

The very idea that we may not be who we think we are, for many people, is something quite revolutionary. This discovery naturally gives rise to the larger question: Is our mind who we are? Are we actually able to be identified by, described by, and defined by the thoughts in our mind? When we begin to look at our experience clearly, we'll see that there are at least two phenomena going on: one is the movement of mind, including all of the descriptions, self-images, ideas, beliefs, and opinions that arise moment to moment. The other phenomenon is the *awareness* of mind. Very rarely do we take into account the awareness of mind, the space in which mind arises and subsides.

Mind has a very powerful ability to put awareness into a trance. Very quickly, we find ourselves lost in that trance. This trance is precisely what we've been calling "egoic consciousness"—the creation of our belief in who we are, which forms the very structure of ego. Ego is nothing more than the beliefs, ideas, and images we have about ourselves—and so it is actually something completely imaginary.

Note what happens to your sense of self when you go to sleep and your mind isn't thinking about who you are. What happens to your beliefs, your ideas and opinions, and the world as you think it is, when you're in bed and asleep? While your mind is resting, none of the projections that your mind imagines exist. All of the imagination of your mind ceases when you go to sleep, at least until you start dreaming. In this state of deep sleep, what you experience is great peace. We call it "sleep," we call it "rest," and it's absolutely vital to our survival. If we don't get enough sleep, we'll eventually go somewhat crazy. We can even die if we don't get enough sleep, if we never allow the mind to come into a deep state of peace and rest, where it isn't thinking anymore.

This is ironic, because we think that if we control our minds in a certain way, then peace, rest, and freedom will be ours. We think that it is simply a matter of coming up with the right thoughts, the right ideas, the right beliefs, then we'll find the key to peace, and from there we will all begin to get along with each other. But our history shows us—hundreds, thousands, tens of thousands of years of history—that our ideas haven't saved us. Our ideas haven't saved us from our own anger, bitterness, and violence. They haven't saved us from wars and famine and destruction. If our history has shown us anything—the history of thought, the history of ideas—it's that thought can't save humanity, that thought can't save the world, that it's going to take something other than even the greatest ideas that we can imagine. Instead, we must start with our own minds. Because if we don't start with ourselves, then our mind is just going to keep projecting itself into the way we view life, and we'll be lost within another dream, another trance.

THE TRANCE OF EGO

As soon as we're caught in a trance state, we're imprisoned in a mechanical, conditioned movement of mind. Everyone knows what it's like to be caught in this egoic trance state: We experience great frustration and dissatisfaction. Part of our frustration arises because the ego can't really do anything about this underlying discontent, because the ego itself is simply a mechanical movement of thought. It can't express any true creativity. Our egos are basically the past expressing itself in the present. By that, I mean the ego is simply our conditioning unfolding and displaying itself here and now—in the way we think, act, and react. In the egoic state of consciousness, we really don't have the amount of choice or volition that we imagine we have.

On a deep, intuitive level, we all know this, because if we had the choice that we think we possess, we would simply choose happiness and peace; nobody who's not insane would choose otherwise. And yet, even though we believe that we have this power of choice, life keeps showing us that we can't even manipulate where our minds go, that we can't even insist on the way we feel day to day, much less control every one of our behaviors or the behaviors of those around us. How many times have we made New Year's resolutions about how we were going to change, and how many times did that change actually occur? More often than not, even the things we say we want to do, we don't end up doing. The reason isn't because we have a lack of willpower. The reason isn't because we haven't figured out how to do them. The reason is because, from the egoic level of consciousness, we don't really have the power of choice that we imagine we have, and that's one of the most frustrating things within the trance state of egoic consciousness.

This trance state of egoic consciousness is where 99 percent of humanity lives and breathes, yet it's the very thing from which we yearn to escape. Even though we don't know it's what we long to be free of, we all have this desire to not be confined or limited imprinted within us. We all have this innate desire to be free, creative, loving, open, and compassionate—and yet when we're trapped within the egoic state of consciousness, in this trance of ego, our options are very limited.

TRANSMUTED THOUGHTS

Egoic consciousness isn't just a mental phenomenon. The ego also holds tightly onto emotions and feelings, and also onto a general sort of energetic quality that goes along with this egoic trance. The content of our thinking produces many of the emotions and feelings that we experience. In a sense, our physical and emotional bodies are duplicating machines for our thoughts. In other words, our bodies turn thoughts into emotions and feelings. It's almost like turning water into wine; it's an alchemical miracle that our bodies can be duplicators for our thoughts. On one side, there's the content of thinking; but in our bodies, from our neck down, thinking arises as feeling, emotion, and sensation. I'm not saying that all of our emotions or all of our feelings are derived from thought, but probably at least 90 percent of them originate there.

Not only have we been taught to identify with the content of our thinking, but we've also been taught to identify with a certain emotional environment. Every human being has an inner environment that makes them feel like they're themselves. It doesn't have to be a particularly positive feeling; some people are identified with a very dense, heavy state of suffering, but when they feel that heavy state of suffering, they feel most like themselves. Everybody has their own unique emotional environment—somewhat like an emotional North Pole. Not only are we taught to identify with the content of our thinking, but we're also taught to identify with how we feel. We are also taught to recognize people in terms of their most common emotional states.

We say it every day in our common language: "I am angry," "I am sad," or "He is an angry person," or "She often seems sad." By believing this about ourselves and others, we literally go into a trance with every feeling and every emotion we have.

THE VORTEX OF SUFFERING

This quality of trance, of being hypnotized, is the hallmark of our egoic state of consciousness. Over millennia, the great spiritual masters of all traditions have realized this and given us many profound teachings about this condition. In one way or another, they all refer to this egoic state of consciousness as a dream, as something that doesn't really exist, but is only imagined to exist. The Buddha called it "the wheel of *Samsara*." He likened it to a spinning wheel of the mind, and as soon as we identify with any thought on that wheel—any image, any idea—the identification pulls us right into this cyclic pattern of suffering, confusion, and contraction.

I like to use a different word for what the Buddha called "the wheel of suffering." To me, it is like a vortex, an energy pattern that, as soon as we get too close to it, as soon as we buy into it, we get caught. This vortex has its own gravitational force that always exists as a potential. The power of that force is not always manifest—we're not always stuck in sorrow, pain, or anger—but the potential for the vortex to arise and for us to get caught in it is very strong. The most common way that this vortex sucks us in is through emotionally based reactions like anger, greed, pride, hate, defensiveness, and the desire for control. These qualities are aspects of our emotional life that pull us right into this vortex of suffering.

The clearest expression of how this vortex works is in the realm of our relationships. We exist in a world of continuous relationship; everywhere you look, everywhere we go, we are in relationship. Every feeling you have is actually one that involves relationship: your body with its environment; your mind with your consciousness; the world outside and the world inside; the relationship of your heart beating at this very moment and your lungs breathing in and out. This is the world of relationship. Of course we have relationships with other human beings, too, and this is where we easily get pulled into this vortex of sorrow and suffering, because as soon as we start to believe thoughts that cause us to feel angry or greedy or frustrated or out of control, we get pulled into the hypnotizing vortex of sorrow and suffering. When we're in relationship and two people get pulled into this vortex, the cycle of conflict and misunderstanding really strengthens, as well as the perceived need to defend, control, and blame the other. It is a very difficult cycle to break free from. The key is to begin by looking closely at your own experience and identifying which thoughts pull you into suffering and which beliefs tend to bring you into conflict.

There are a few important things to understand about this vortex of suffering. Again, I use the word "vortex" because the trance of our minds is very much like a swirling locus of energy. Like an energetic vacuum cleaner, it can suck your consciousness right into it, very quickly. In every moment, the vortex has the potential to arise very suddenly and pull you in. What feeds the vortex are emotionally laden reactions like anger, pride, and fear, as well as the ego's desire to control, to exercise power, and to make demands. All of these are energies that exist in potential within our egoic structure, and as soon as we believe in them, or buy into their seductive qualities, we instantly find ourselves having been sucked into the vortex.

The egoic state of consciousness is comprised almost entirely of this vortex and, as such, you can see its manifestations all around you. If you listen to people interact, at the very instant they get sucked into the vortex, you'll hear them start to blame, condemn, or try to control each other. Or it might be something a bit more subtle, where they'll be very quietly trying to convince each other of their point of view. Brought into the vortex, one might then move into a place of withdrawal or victimhood or neediness. It's important to see, from an egoic state of consciousness, that many of the qualities that pull us into the vortex are qualities of mind and emotion that our egos find very valuable. Most egos think it's important to have control over others, over the environment, and of course over our lives. It seems so obvious that one would want to have some amount of control over their experience. Yet, the irony is, the more you try to control life and others, the more out of control you feel. This feeling of being out of control is in fact the swirling energy of this vortex of suffering itself. You're caught in it, and once you're caught in it you'll tend to try to grasp for more control as a means of getting out, and you'll only dig yourself in deeper and deeper.

Remember, you can get trapped within this vortex when you are by yourself, in your own thoughts, and you can also get entangled in relationship. Much of what we learn, much of what's been modeled to us about how to be in relationship, are the very qualities of mind and emotion that pull us into the vortex. We spend lifetimes listening to people trying to convince each other that they're right. We see people using anger, power, and control to manipulate others, and we see that sometimes, on the surface of things, this kind of manipulation seems to work out for the person using it. Of course, in the end, whatever we attain through power, manipulation, and control is something that ultimately makes us internally suffer and feel powerless, craving for more and more control.

YOUR OWN MIND IS THE PLACE TO START

There are ways that you can avoid being sucked into the vortex of suffering and sorrow—and in any given moment, whether you are alone or in relationship, you have the opportunity to evade the vortex. Your own mind is always the best place to start. It will be very easy for us to be caught and sucked into suffering when we haven't first dealt with and understood how our own minds can pull us into the vortex. Even when things are going our way, eventually everything changes and shifts; the ego has a way of coming up with some reason to suffer eventually. At some point, despite how well things seem to be going, it will come up with a reason to contract.

One of the curious reasons why the ego always brings us back to suffering is that, strangely enough, our ego actually has to be in some resistance to what is. Otherwise, our sense of separation begins to dissolve, we move from our head into our heart and go from a place where we think we know into a very soft space in the heart. From the egoic point of view, it's vital that we remain in conflict to some extent, and that's why, when we look at the world around us, we see so much conflict among human beings. It's not just because conflict is inevitable. It's because, as long as we're stuck in the egoic state of consciousness, we're extraordinarily prone to be pulled into this vortex of suffering, because the ego needs the vortex to maintain its sense of separation and to survive. When you watch the mind, you will notice that it is always trying to make itself separate. It is expert at drawing distinctions and pitting itself, in one way or another, against something or someone else. And the more deeply we're in a trance, the less likely it will be that we'll even consider that we might be in a trance. The ego is very intelligent that way. This is the dilemma that human beings have been in for thousands of years: collectively caught in a trance state of ego and thus prone to being sucked into this vortex of suffering and sorrow.

The opportunity to wake up out of this egoic trance, to break out of the vortex of suffering, is something that, historically speaking, has been reserved for a select few. In the past, it was only a small minority who looked at themselves and their minds in a profoundly deep way. These were the great mystics and masters of the past, those who felt a deep call to move beyond the egoic state of consciousness. They felt the suffering inherent in the state of consciousness that most human beings exist in, and for some reason, they were compelled to move beyond it with enough force and enough drive that they actually succeeded. Today, this same invitation, this same yearning, this same necessity is calling out to all of us. It's no longer something that's reserved for the mystics, for just a very few, because our collective survival depends on our consciousness awakening from this dream of separation and isolation.

THE ORDINARY NATURE OF AWAKENING

As I travel, I meet people just like you and me—very ordinary people—who are being called to explore the nature of their hearts and minds in order to find a response to the confusion and suffering that we all experience. They're called in a way that the mystics of the past were called, and even though they're not monks or nuns, *sadhus* or renunciants, they nonetheless are feeling and expressing this very authentic spiritual yearning for transformation. They lead normal, ordinary lives—going to work and raising their children—and what I am finding is that more and more people are actually beginning to wake up from this trance state of ego, from this state of suffering that has been held together because of the way we cling to our beliefs, opinions, and ideas.

For almost everyone, opening to the possibility that we can let go of our ideas, beliefs, and opinions brings up a lot of resistance and fear. It is actually quite threatening: Who would I be without my beliefs? Who would I be if I didn't grasp onto my opinions? Who would I be if I wasn't looking for others and outside circumstances to bring me the happiness and freedom I am yearning for? Who would I be if I fell into the center of my own consciousness? Who would I be if I fell into the heart, not as some sort of ideal, not as something I imagine, but something that I actually allow to happen at the deepest level?

Historically as well as today, people think that spiritual awakening—which is nothing more than waking up from the egoic state of consciousness—is reserved for the very few and that achieving this liberation from suffering is extraordinarily difficult. These thoughts of difficulty or rareness—which are, after all, only beliefs in the mind—are perhaps the most powerful reasons why so few people have embarked on a path to transform their own consciousness. If we look closely, we can see that these thoughts of how rare spiritual awakening is, that only special people can truly awaken, are just beliefs held in the mind. Transformation and awakening are available to everyone. If we grasp onto and identify with the notion that awakening isn't possible for us, then we are literally shut off from the possibility of it.

As soon as we begin to transform the ideas we have of ourselves, we get out of our own way, and a door then opens to who and what we really are. We all have this natural yearning for happiness and freedom. At the core, none of us wants to suffer. When our hearts begin to open, it becomes clear that none of us wants to cause anyone else to suffer, either.

THE EGO'S ADDICTION TO PAIN AND STRUGGLE

Make no mistake about it: Egos are addicted to pain. They're addicted to struggle. In fact, egos tend to bond, in some part, through pain and struggle. When you have a conversation with somebody—a friend or a stranger—and they tell you the most wonderful, glorious thing that ever happened to them in their life, you'll probably be interested. You'll probably listen, and maybe you'll even celebrate with them. But if you're like most people, when that same person tells you the worst, most terrible thing that ever happened, you'll start listening even closer. It's like you're being pulled into the reality of that person's inner life. This is very telling. Egos tend to bond in pain, not in happiness.

I'm not saying there's no happiness at all in the egoic state of consciousness; of course, even while within it, we can and do experience moments of happiness, joy, and relative peace. So it wouldn't be true to suggest that to be caught within the imagination of ego is all bad. If it was all bad, nobody would remain caught for long. Part of the challenge is that the experience of being led by our egos is both good *and* bad. There are times when you're very accepting of life, and there are times when you're very rejecting of life. This back and forth of acceptance and rejection, of pushing and pulling, of "I love" and "I hate," this is what keeps our consciousness caught in the ego, and this is what makes us so prone to being sucked into the vortex of suffering.

But we all have the seed of awakening within us. This awakening does not require you to totally disengage from your mind or even from your ego. The very notion that there is something you need to get rid of is a notion that belongs to the mind, to the ego itself, because minds and egos divide life. What I'm speaking about is not division at all. You are simply being invited to wake up from a trance. The less you push your mind away, the easier it is to wake up from it. The conflict of getting frustrated with your mind, your suffering, is what holds your mind in a limited view of things. It doesn't matter why you're in conflict. It doesn't matter what you're denying. It doesn't matter what in yourself you're struggling to change. The mere fact that you're struggling guarantees that your consciousness will not be able to wake up from its state of limitation.

LETTING GO OF YOUR ARGUMENT WITH WHAT IS

Sometimes, when things get bad enough, when the suffering gets deep enough or intense enough, the whole egoic wheel stops spinning. It becomes too painful to identify with the conditioned thoughts in your head and with the chronic painful reactions that are associated with them. And when the vortex stops, and you are right in the middle of the greatest grief, right in the middle of the greatest torment and suffering, something else may dawn on you. A sense of peace and freedom may be felt at that moment, and it shows you that nothing really needs to change. You don't need to struggle against yourself. Just the opposite. All you need is the willingness to question your mind's conclusions, the willingness to just relax. Instead of trying to change now, just let now be as it is, even though your mind may have plenty of reasons why you should resist it. Try it anyway.

What happens when you let go of your argument with what is? No matter how you're feeling—whether you're feeling good or anxious, happy or sad, conflicted or free—just let it be. Experiment to see what happens when you stop being in conflict with yourself. When you let go of conflict, even for a moment, there's a natural stopping. In the moment you're not in conflict with yourself, in the moment where you're willing to no longer be in opposition to anything, you come completely into now, into this moment. What you'll begin to experience is a peace and a stillness—a deep inner quietness. At that moment, you're experiencing a whole different dimension of consciousness, one beyond the ego and its activity.

Many people think that this dimension of consciousness of peace, stillness, and well-being is something for which you have to work very hard to attain—that somehow it's far away and that you must earn it in some way. But all these conclusions are just more thoughts in the mind, so as with all thoughts, you can choose to no longer grasp at them. You can open to a state of being where there are no conclusions, where your mind is wide open, where your consciousness is at ease, and where you can begin to touch upon a whole new dimension of consciousness, a consciousness that actually is at peace. It's an invitation to just be, to *be* that consciousness, and also to act from it. Once you taste this stillness, this peace, then the ego will stand out in stark contrast to it. The vortex of suffering will then be much easier to see. You may go unconscious for moments, you may not always see the ego trying to hijack you with various thoughts, but even when that happens, if you just stop for a moment and see the pattern, then a gap opens up. It's a doorway to a different possibility—a possibility to experience the peace and happiness for which you've always been longing—even when you are right in the middle of conflict.

FINDING FREEDOM EVEN IN THE MOST DIFFICULT MOMENTS

When I was in my mid-twenties, I had a beautiful dog. I'm sure some of you have had pets that you deeply loved. I had this wonderful dog, and he was a constant companion. He went with me everywhere. Any room I went to in the house, he followed me. Anywhere I went in the car, he was my companion. We were together almost all the time. And then he developed a form of epilepsy, at which time I took him to the vet. They tried to give him medication to treat it, but the question of how much medication to take or not take is sort of an art. We were just starting to treat him, and after a few weeks, I came home, and he was in the midst of an epileptic fit. And the fit didn't stop. It went on and on and on, and there was no way to save him. Eventually, he ended up having to be put down. This was one of the saddest moments in my life. Prior to that moment, I'd experienced some amount of grief in my life. I've had grandparents die and friends die, and sometimes people very close to me die, but I was never affected like I was when I lost this great companion. I found myself in deep sorrow—a sorrow that I couldn't really understand, because I'd never experienced it before.

One afternoon, some friends, family, and I went out in the back yard for a final goodbye. I had my dog's collar and a few other things that had belonged to him, and we put them in a box. I had written out what I wanted to say, and as I began to read his eulogy, I began to weep—tears just started pouring out of my eyes. At some point, the grief was so immense that I decided to just completely give in to it. I completely let go into this great well of sorrow and grief. I was crying and crying, while still trying to continue with the eulogy. And then something very mysterious happened, something that I didn't expect at all: right in the middle of this immense grief and sadness, right at the point of the heart in my chest, there was this very small pinprick of light. And right in the midst of this pinprick of light, there was a smile. I could literally almost see a smile in my mind in this pinprick of light.

When it started, it was just a small point within this vast expanse of grief and sorrow. But as I kept crying, as I kept speaking the eulogy, this point of happiness began to expand. After a few minutes, this point of happiness had vastly grown and become absolutely immense, and there was this very strange, paradoxical experience. On one hand, I was enmeshed in this deep state of grief and sadness. But at the very same moment, there was a greater happiness and a greater sense of well-being than I'd ever experienced in my life.

It was one of the most profound experiences I'd ever had. What it revealed to me was that even in the deepest states of darkness, even in the most intense states of loss, grief, or depression, we can find some measure of happiness and well-being when we really open to the difficult feelings, when we really let go of our resistance, when we completely let go of trying to contain those painful experiences, when we finally just allow them to be there, to be as overwhelming as they may want to be. The peace and happiness can arise when we profoundly let go, when we really decide to stop struggling.

I've told this story many times, and I've received many letters and cards from people who've shared similar experiences. I received a letter from one person who had been lost in a deep depression for decades, until one day she decided to stop—to stop struggling, to stop trying to push it away, but also to stop indulging in it, to stop feeding it—just to simply stop. In the moment of stopping, something completely unexpected was born: the opposite showed up. As deep as her depression was, there arose this sense of well-being when it was met fully. It's not like the depression just went away and disappeared forever, but it began to exist simultaneously within a field of absolute well-being. When the depression exists within a state of well-being, one is not overwhelmed anymore. As time went on, at least for this person, the depression began to wane. It's as if the depression had something to give itself up to; it could let go into well-being.

This phenomena of finding well-being amidst the difficult isn't something that most people have experienced, because they haven't really ever stopped trying to grasp at or push away a certain quality of thinking and feeling. If you just completely surrender to the emotions or thoughts, you will see the invitation there, the invitation to wake up from your idea of yourself and the whole emotional environment with which you identify. There is a way that you can really stop. The truth is that a whole new state of consciousness already exists, that every part of your experience that's unfolding right now is already enclosed within absolute stillness, absolute ease. And so there really isn't anywhere to go or anything for which to search. Struggle only gets us deeper into the very thing we're trying to escape. This is a very important thing to know about egoic consciousness: The harder we try to get out, the deeper we dig ourselves in.

* * *

The invitation is simple: Let go of indulging in the mind, realize it doesn't have the answers for you, and it doesn't have the answers for us collectively. Together we can begin to stop the insanity within ourselves and amongst each other. Realizing our deep, essential nature and finding the peace and happiness that lie there is not just something for ourselves; it's a gift to all of humanity. Because when we begin to become expressions of what's possible for anybody and everybody, we are contributing to the goodness at the very core of who each and everyone is. When we can relate to ourselves from stillness, from a place before the mind, then we can begin to relate to each other from that same place. Initially it might seem quite difficult to relate to someone else without getting pulled back into the egoic mind, back into the egoic consciousness, or even into the vortex of suffering, but if you simply hold that as your intention, it will start to happen—maybe all at once, maybe bit by bit.

There's really nothing to learn here. Awakening is actually a process of unlearning. The important thing is where we're acting from, where we're relating from. When we relate from our true spiritual essence, then the quality of our relating is transformed. Then what we say to each other carries a whole different feel to it. It is then that we become expressions of peace, rather than expressions of the insanity of a divided world. This revelation begins with the recognition that you are not your mind, and you are not your ego or your personality. In fact, you are something much, much vaster.

4

Letting Go of Struggle

SINCE OUR IMMERSION in the egoic state of consciousness is ultimately the cause of all our suffering, it's essential that we begin to shift our consciousness. We must awaken to our natural state: who we really are. In order to do this, it's important to set the groundwork from which awakening naturally springs. First we have to see that our normal state of egoic consciousness is a state where we tend to struggle. I'm not necessarily referring here to dense, overwhelming struggling, those moments in life of intense suffering— though this would be included as well. I'm referring to even our more subtle struggling. But you can't just tell somebody to stop struggling. You can't just say, "Okay, struggling is a big part of your problem, so all you have to do is let go of struggling." So after we see that we struggle, we must next try to understand *why* it is that we struggle, why it is that we fight against what is. Because, after all, that's what struggling is based on: a fighting against what is, or what was, or what may be in the future.

When we struggle, we manufacture something in our experience that, to the egoic state of consciousness, is very essential: a contraction. A "contraction" is simply a narrowing down. When you feel a contraction in your body—whether it's in your stomach, your heart, or even in your head—you experience a narrowing down, a squeezing in. When we're contracted, we're actually pulled out of wholeness, out of a sense of completeness, and into a sense of being small or separate.

Struggle is necessary in order to stay in the egoic state of consciousness, and that's why, when you look at the world around you, you see so much struggling. The reason that we struggle to maintain the egoic state is because it allows us to live our lives as if we are in control and separate from the world around us. While ultimately this proves to be very unsatisfying, it does provide a certain amount of comfort and security, and it allows us to stay in the known and not venture too much into unknown territory.

So there is struggling at all levels. Whether it's at work, in our politics, in our families, or even in our friendships, there's often some element of struggle. Struggle is that feeling, that tension, when we're working against something. It might mean opposition with another human being, with an institution, or often, within ourselves—where one part of ourselves is pitted against another. It's the struggle of trying to be who we wish we were. As soon as we have that kind of division in our minds, we begin to struggle, and as long as we're struggling, it's very hard for consciousness to shift out of the egoic state, into something more natural, expansive, and whole.

This natural and expansive state is really just another word for "spirit." Though this word is quite loaded and used in a variety of ways, it in essence points to the vast expanse of consciousness that is possible for all of us. What is spirit, after all? It's not something you can see. It's nothing you can grasp. It's nothing you can really touch. Another way to describe spirit is as an "awake nothing." One of the terms I especially like from the Bible is "Holy Ghost," because to me, spirit is like a ghost—not because it's frightening, but because it's an invisible, ungraspable something without real definition. A ghost is something that exists without really existing, and spirit is like that—an awake nothingness, an awake expanse of consciousness. In contrast, the egoic state of consciousness is nothing more than a narrowing down of spirit, a contraction of this vast expanse. When that spiritual consciousness contracts and narrows down, it eventually starts to feel separate.

The way we narrow down consciousness is through struggling, through striving. What we all aspire to, and what is in fact natural to us, is openness, peace, love, and well-being. These qualities are completely natural qualities of spirit. They arise in us when we become conscious of our spiritual nature, of our non-separate, non-somebody nature. Then love flows quite naturally.

I can remember when I started to have this yearning for truth, this yearning to end the struggle and to feel whole and complete. For me, the question to which I kept returning was, "What's real? What's true?" Somehow I intuited that if I could just find what's real and what's true, I would discover clarity and liberation in my life. The truth would allow me to be openhearted and free. And yet, even as I was seeking that openness and freedom, the way that I was seeking it was through struggle itself. I didn't know I was struggling, but I was. Most of the people I meet who are seeking happiness, freedom, or liberation, are actually going about it in a way in which they're unconsciously struggling. When I became aware of this desire for freedom, when it became conscious in me, I began to spend more time sitting in silence. I was reading many books on freedom and liberation at the time and they all seemed to say the same thing: "You need to be quiet. You need to quiet your mind, because if you don't quiet your mind, you can't see beyond it." So I spent hours and hours sitting quietly, trying to calm my mind. The problem was that this kind of trying involved great effort. I spent many years struggling to get beyond the mind.

I think this is actually quite common, not only in spiritual circles in which people meditate a lot, but also in daily life. Many people are trying to calm their minds or calm their emotions, and in the process of trying to do this there is tension inside, an internal struggle. This is one of the things that can be so frustrating, because we all yearn for a sense of wholeness and freedom, and yet we attempt to get there through trying to change ourselves, struggling to alter who and what we are. But struggling is the antithesis of what opens the way for us to awaken from the egoic state of consciousness. So how can we stop struggling? How do we come upon that inner peace where we are no longer fighting against ourselves?

It's usually believed that letting go in this way is a complicated process, requiring some special sort of knowledge or information that we need to understand, that there's some process that needs to unfold or that must happen within us. But really, coming to the end of struggle is easier than that. It's much more obvious, which is why we don't notice it. The truth is hidden right in front of our eyes. It's everywhere we look, but it's hard to see, because we really don't see that clearly. Though it seems like it would be hard not to struggle, it really isn't. What makes it seem hard is that our sense of self, our "little me," is trying to not struggle, and as long as we, as a sense of self, are trying to not struggle, the very intention to do so sets up a tension inside us, a sort of psychological and emotional tightness.

Relaxing and letting go of struggle isn't something that the ego does—yet we often get our egos involved in trying to make letting go happen. To even say, "Let go of struggle," isn't quite right. All that's required is that you begin to notice that place within you that's not struggling. To do this means there's really no future for which to hope. In fact, the idea of the future is one of the barriers of awakening to our true nature. This is because the future keeps us looking at something other than what's happening right now. If you were to ask yourself, "Even before I try to stop struggling, even before I try to relax and find peace, is peace already here?" Then just be quiet for a moment, and listen. We assume that what we're seeking isn't already present. Of course that's why we're seeking it: because we believe that peace and happiness and freedom aren't here, right where we are, right now, already. The assumption that what we're seeking, some state of completion, isn't here right now is what causes us to look for it, to start the search.

STANDING IN YOUR OWN TWO SHOES

The real search isn't a search into tomorrow, or to anywhere other than now. It's starting to look into the very nature of this moment. In order to do that, you have to "stand in your own two shoes," as my teacher used to say. What she meant by "standing in your own two shoes" is you have to look clearly into your own experience. Stop trying to have someone else's experience. Stop chasing freedom or happiness, or even spiritual enlightenment. Stand in your own shoes, and examine closely: What's happening right here and right now? Is it possible to let go of trying to make anything happen? Even in this moment, there may be some suffering, there may be some unhappiness, but even if there is, is it possible to no longer push against it, to try to get rid of it, to try to get somewhere else?

I understand that our instinct is to move away from what's not comfortable, to try to get somewhere better, but as my teacher used to say, "You need to take the backward step, not the forward step." The forward step is always moving ahead, always trying to attain what you want, whether it's a material possession or inner peace. The forward step is very familiar: seeking and more seeking, striving and more striving, always looking for peace, always looking for happiness, looking for love. To take the backward step means to just turn around, reverse the whole process of looking for satisfaction on the outside, and look at precisely the place where you are standing. See if what you are looking for isn't already present in your experience.

So, again, to lay the groundwork for awakening, we must first let go of struggling. You let go by acknowledging that the end of struggle is actually present in your experience now. The end of struggle is peace. Even if your ego is struggling, even if you're trying to figure this out and "do it right," if you really look, you might just see that struggle is happening within a greater context of peace, within an inner stillness. But if you try to make stillness happen, you'll miss it. If you try to make peace happen, you'll miss it. This is more like a process of recognition, giving recognition to a stillness that is naturally present.

We're not bringing struggle to an end. We're not trying to *not* struggle anymore. We're just noticing that there is a whole other dimension to consciousness that, in this very moment, isn't struggling, isn't resentful, isn't trying to get somewhere. You can literally feel it in your body. You can't think your way to not struggling. There isn't a three-point plan of how not to struggle. It's really a one-point plan: Notice that the peace, this end of struggling, is actually already present.

The process is therefore one of recognition. We recognize that there is peace now, even if your mind is confused. You may see that even when you touch upon peace now, the mind is so conditioned to move away from it that it will try to argue with the basic fact of peace's existence within you: "I can't be at peace yet because I have to do this, or that, or this question hasn't been answered, or that question hasn't been answered, or so-and-so hasn't apologized to me." There are all sorts of ways that the egoic mind can insist that something needs to happen, something needs to change, in order for you to be at peace. But this is part of the dream of the mind. We're all taught that something needs to change for us to experience true peace and freedom.

Just imagine for a moment that this isn't true. Even though you may believe that it's true, just imagine for a moment: What would it be like if you didn't need to struggle, if you didn't need to make an effort to find peace and happiness? What would that feel like now? And just take a moment to be quiet and see if peace or stillness is with you in this moment.

WHAT DO WE KNOW WITH ABSOLUTE CERTAINTY?

Another way that we struggle is through our continuous need to know. We want to know "Why this?" and "Why that?" and how to do this and how to do that. In this way, the mind could be likened to a machine with an endless battery supply. It always, always, always wants to know. In many ways, this quality of the mind is quite natural—and at times essential for our survival. It is fine for the mind to seek and possess the kind of knowing that helps us accomplish practical tasks. That's why we go to school and learn things, so that we can pursue our vocations and operate in this world we've created. There's a lot of knowing that's very useful, but when it comes to our state of consciousness, when it comes to finding peace and happiness, we have to let go of knowing. We have to let go of the effort to know, because really, we don't know.

As an experiment, ask yourself this question: "What do I know for certain?" Not "What do I know with 99 percent certainty?" but "What do I know with total certainty, for myself?" When you ask this question and you genuinely look at what arises, first all your ideas will surface—all your opinions, your beliefs, everything you've learned, all the things you think you know, because we do think we know an awful lot of things. And yet all our knowing hasn't prevented us from suffering—individually or collectively. Yet we continue to go back to wanting to know and to working our minds in order to figure out this dilemma of human suffering and find freedom. Can we be honest enough to look directly at the nature of our own mind and ask, "What do we really know?"

All the knowing in our minds, as I mentioned before, is symbolic, which means every thought we have is merely a symbol for something. Whether it's the word "book" or "tree" or "shoe" or "shirt," these are all symbols that point toward something else. Of course, some of our thoughts don't even do that. They just point to other thoughts—thinking about thinking.

THERE IS NO SUCH THING AS A TRUE THOUGHT

Part of coming to the end of struggle is seeing that we don't really know most of what we think we know. This is a really big step. By "a big step," I don't mean it's difficult, but it is a big shift in how we've come to understand the world, in our consciousness. I can remember when this shift happened for me. At the time, I worked at a machine shop with my father. I was leaving work, and I was walking into the parking lot, toward my car, at the end of the day. The funny thing is that I really wasn't thinking about anything in particular. But all of a sudden, what came into my mind, the thought that I had, was that there's no such thing as a true thought.

But this observation wasn't just a thought that came into my head. It was more like what I might call an "insight." A true insight isn't just a thought that arises in your mind. An insight is something that you understand and comprehend with your entire body. That's why, when you have an insight, you often say, "Aha!" It's the "Aha!" which is the response of your body. When you have a regular thought, there's no sense of "Aha!" An everyday, every-moment kind of thought is actually dissociated from your body. An insight, on the other hand, involves a deep understanding with our entire being. It's a great moment of revelation, an experience on the intellectual, emotional, and kinesthetic levels.

So, all at once, this knowledge was delivered: "Oh my gosh! There's no such thing as a true thought!" It was so stunning that I immediately proclaimed, "I have to think about this!" A strange response, to be sure, but it seemed so irrational, so unreasonable, that there would be no such thing as a true thought. How could that possibly be? But when I began to look at this insight, I saw that thoughts are symbols for things; they're not the things, themselves. They're descriptions of things. I began to see the truth that thought doesn't have any reality to it; in other words, a mentally formed conclusion isn't the truth. This is a very revolutionary thing to come to. It appeared as revolutionary to me at the time, as well, to see that none of my thoughts are true. And I do mean *see*, because realization or revelation has the quality of *seeing*—you see something all at once. That was the "Aha!" "There's no such thing as a true thought." What a surprise!

Some thoughts are useful, others seem to be quite useless, but whether a thought is useful or useless, relevant or irrelevant, intelligent or unintelligent, still no thought is ultimately true. If you see that no thought is ultimately true, then you can stop looking to your mind to tell you what's real. Where do we look, then? If I'm not going to look into my mind for truth, where am I going to look? If I'm not going to ask my thoughts what is real, then to whom am I going to ask the question? How am I ever going to find what's real and true if I don't think about it?

With any good "Aha!" moment or revelation, everything comes to a halt. For a moment, it stuns you. In that moment in which I realized that no thought is true, all other thoughts became irrelevant. They didn't mean anything. They were just the mind trying to describe something, to tell a story. We love to tell each other stories, we love to tell ourselves stories, and above all, our mind loves to tell stories to itself, to create fictions about what we receive through our sense impressions. But if we allow this idea that no thought is actually real or true to sink into the core of our being, we can begin this complete shift in consciousness. Because if no thought is true, then you'll no longer believe any thought that causes you to struggle.

ENTERING INTO THE HEART OF REALITY

I heard a great physicist on a radio program just a few weeks ago, and he said something quite amazing for a scientist: "You know, even in quantum mechanics, our theories don't really tell us what's true and what's real. They just explain the behaviors of things. They're symbols for reality. They're not really real." I was amazed! Here's a scientist, who spends his whole life attempting to make clear and precise concepts, and what he's saying is none of those concepts, none of those formulas, are ultimately real. They're useful, yes; they may explain certain parts of the functioning of the world, but in and of themselves, they're not real. Now, if a scientist can say that, then you and I can at least be open to this observation that what we think isn't really true.

But when you open yourself to this notion that all your ideas aren't true, you're likely to feel quite empty-handed. The mind doesn't know quite what to do. It feels exposed and vulnerable. It's very likely that your mind has never been in this place before, and you might feel the mind's compulsive desire to know. That's okay, because it's part of the function of the mind to try to know, to tell stories about the way things are. But the stories will never be as true as the way things really are. So just take a moment and feel your mind and its innate desire to know, to conceive, to tell a story. None of our stories, even our most intelligent stories, are ever as real as what is.

Beyond this feeling of empty-handedness, beyond this void of not knowing, there is something greater: the heart of reality. The heart of reality isn't just a rarified insight that we "bring back from the mountaintop," so to speak. It isn't a concept. The heart of reality is a vast expanse that we actually live in. What if we began to relate to each other from this place where we know that our thoughts aren't ultimately true, but we're still going to use them? We're still going to communicate, aren't we? We're still going to tell each other stories. But wouldn't it be revolutionary if, even as we were telling each other stories, we knew that they were only approximations of what's true, at best, while most of our stories don't even approximate the truth very well at all? Can you imagine how much more lightly you'd hold your mind, the next thought in your mind, the thought that tries to convince you to struggle? What would happen if your mind were disarmed? What would happen if you suddenly realized that happiness, peace, love, and freedom weren't going to come from your mind?

Look in this moment, and you'll see: The things we value most in life—happiness, love, creativity, peace, joy, union—even though I can reference these by using a thought, none of them are actually the same as the thought. I'm sure you can see and feel that love is something that transcends the word "love." Just to say "love" is to point to an idea. But what's the feeling? What does it feel like to have your heart open? What does it feel like to let your boundaries down? What does it feel like to become intimate with this very moment? Can that be put into an idea? When you really feel love, isn't it the case that you don't actually know how to express it in words or with thought? When you feel this love, you've entered the heart of reality—and this is the space from which you can live when you let go of the belief that all our thoughts, all our ideas, are true.

SILENCE IS THE GROUND FROM WHICH AWAKENING SPRINGS

The one common thing about any true revelation is that it will stun our mind, because at that moment, we comprehend something that's not just in thought. Revelation and insight come from somewhere else, from some other space. They come from a place that we as a culture seem to have so little respect for—a place called "silence." What's more neglected in our lives than silence? What do we run away from more than silence? Many of us would rather cling to our ideas, our beliefs, and our opinions—the very things that distance us from truth and reality and life—than to experience this silence. We spend so much energy running away from silence, but silence is the ground from which awakening springs. It's the ground from which we shift out of this egoic state of consciousness, out of this belief in separation. After all, separation is ultimately just a belief. It's a story made up in our minds.

I'm not saying that we have to try to *become* quiet, that we have to practice stillness. If you really want to become quiet and still, simply allow yourself to see that all of the thoughts in your head are just stories. They're not good or bad stories. They're not right or wrong. Our mind is a storyteller—and it keeps us removed from the silence, the quiet, that is always present. Often, our minds are really good storytellers—and other times really poor storytellers—but ultimately, the mind just tells stories. And a story isn't real; it isn't actually true.

Silence is something that disarms us, which is why we move away from it so often. Our society is one in which we're more and more preoccupied with noise. Last week, I was driving down the highway, and I looked over and saw a group of high school kids walking home from school. They all had cell phones. There were seven or eight of them, and every single one of them was either talking on their phone or texting. No one was interacting with the people or the environment around them. I thought, "This is crazy! Here's this group of people walking home together, but not actually connecting."

We've gotten to a point where we're so intimidated by silence and the present moment before us that even when we're together we try our best to make sure that we're very busy. We're physically together without actually being together! We'll walk home together, but we'll talk to somebody else. We're doubly occupied, just to make sure there's no real silence, no real communion. This isn't a bad thing. I'm not even saying it shouldn't happen. I'm just saying that if we look at the world around us, we see that we are conditioned to not listen deeply. Because isn't that what silence is? It's a listening. It's a deep, wordless listening. As one wise Christian mystic said, "Stop telling God what you want, and instead listen to what God has to say to you." That's a very wise thing to say, and it comes from a basic insight into how our minds incessantly assert themselves, which ultimately is just another form of struggle.

So there are all these various ways that we struggle with ourselves and our experiences, trying to control life and those around us. The ways that we struggle keep us locked and confined within the prison of the ego. When we begin to see that our mind is just a storyteller, however, then we begin to listen—not for more thoughts or more complicated understandings, but for the silence. It is when you listen in this way that you can see that it is only your mind that has the capacity to make you suffer. Only your mind has the capacity to convince you to struggle. Only your mind, nothing else. It's all an inside job. It's all happening inside you.

THE UNKNOWN IS OUR DOORWAY

In order to see through the mind and the deeply ingrained sense of separation that continues to generate so much confusion and suffering in our lives, we must take a chance; we must leave what we know and enter that mysterious reality of the unknown. The unknown is a very intimate place. You may feel very exposed when you open yourself to this inner space of unknowing, but really, the unknown is our only doorway. It's by allowing ourselves to not know that we can become truly sensitive, open, and available. It's the most humbling thing in the world to admit that we don't know, to surrender to the fact that we can't know the nature of reality with our minds. This realization is what opens the way for us: the way to the greatest knowing is through not knowing.

As the great mystic Saint John of the Cross said, "In order to come to the knowledge you have not, you must go by a way in which you know not." I love this quote. It's entirely paradoxical. It is what I spoke about earlier in what my teacher referred to as "the backward step": coming to knowledge not through knowing, but through not knowing.

Once you get to the frontier of your mind, to its farthest outreach, you'll come to a place where you can't go any further, where the next thought would just take you back into the mind rather than beyond it. When most people get to this point, they either turn back into their mind, or they just start to move along this imaginary frontier, imagining what it would be like to move beyond it. This is the doorway to the place beyond suffering.

When you find yourself at this boundary of your mind, when you've gone to that place where you realize that you can't go any deeper within the mind, then you begin to stop. You begin to let go. You begin to embrace this unknowing. Embracing the unknown makes us wonderfully and beautifully humble—not humiliated, but truly humble. True humility is a very open state. It's a state of great availability, and it's from this state of great availability and openness, from this willingness to realize how little we really know, that our consciousness begins to shift. It begins to shift from the mind and ego into its natural state. By "natural"

I mean something that's not conceived, something that's not staged or altered, something that doesn't take effort to maintain. In order to find the end of struggle, we have to find a state of consciousness that's totally natural, that doesn't fight against our inner or outer environment. That's what I call "aware spirit," or "awake spirit." It's an awake emptiness. That may sound abstract, but simply put it's the openness to a lived sense of not knowing. What are you when you don't define yourself? What becomes of the past, of the present, or of the future when you don't go into your mind to think about it? It's not so difficult to have a taste of this, to get a feel for this openness and ease. But don't be satisfied with just a fleeting moment of this state of being. This is the doorway in. Dive fully into this openness and avail yourself of the intimacy found there, in not knowing.

WHO YOU ARE BEFORE YOU WERE BORN

There's a wonderful quote from the Gospel of Thomas in which Jesus says, "Blessed is he who existed before being born." Jesus is pointing here to *being* itself; he is acknowledging that essence of who and what we are before our minds created an image of ourselves as something separate and distinct from all of life. Truthfully, we can't imagine what we were before we were born. We can tell ourselves a story about it, or propose a theory about it, but this is not what Jesus was referencing. Before you took form, before you took shape, before you were an infant in your mother's womb, before your parents came together, what were you?

Generally, our minds are so cluttered with ideas about who and what we are that we are unable to touch in on this truth of being, although most of us do have a feeling about this part of ourselves. We have some vague sense that we're something other than we're pretending to be. When we pretend, there is a deeply rooted feeling that something is missing; we can see that every image we have of ourselves is deficient at its core.

We very rarely confess this feeling of insufficiency to one other. We keep it a secret out of the fear that we are the only ones who feel this way. We think everyone else is quite clear about who and what they are; however, if you really ask people, and if they are willing to be genuinely open, they'll tell you, "Yes, I've felt this uncertainty, too." They'll share with you that they've touched this realization of how the identity they've created for themselves doesn't really capture the feeling, the essence, of who they are in their lives. They'll admit that often it feels as if they are acting in a play. Many of us go through life in this way. We're playing a part that we learned how to play, but the problem is that we don't know how to "un-play" it. We think we need another part, perhaps a better part. But really, is that true? What would happen if for a moment we stopped and didn't play *any* part, if we allowed ourselves to be un-born and to touch upon who and what we were before we took form, before we appeared to be someone distinct and different?

If you stop in this place of not knowing who you are, if you resist the temptation to conceptualize an identity, you'll begin to touch a lived sense of an inner presence.

You'll open to what I call an "alive, pregnant nothingness." This is not a "nothingness" that is blank or absent of any qualities, but rather one that is extraordinarily vital and rich with potential. Here we can enter a mysterious dimension that is not accessible through our normal routes of thinking and understanding; we can see clearly that what we are isn't something we can think about. We can only think about what we're not. What we are in reality is alive, awake, and conscious, existing as pure potential.

From this place of pure potential and alive presence, we come into the world of form. We are birthed into the world. Our form develops in the womb of our mother as we journey from a vast expanse of emptiness into the physical dimension. This form with which we begin to identify, a merely physical form, is actually something immense that develops out of this pure potential. After nine months, from this warm, comfortable womb, there you are! The suddenness of being birthed into this life is quite a shock. It's such a shock that spirit, which is open and free, immediately contracts and grasps onto the body, just like you grab onto someone when you're at a movie theater and you become frightened. Consciousness also does this when you're first born. It's such a change of environment that spirit grabs hold of the body, and at that moment identification begins.

It is possible that this entire process of birth into the world of form could be seen in a different way. Yes, birth into form happens, and there is a vivid appearance of a body-mind; a beautiful, wonderful, unimaginably creative display. We witness spirit masquerading as a body in a form that contains a mind, senses, and feelings. But as we look very closely, we perceive that there is nothing about this form, this body, that is in any way separate from where it came, the source in spirit.

Even through this process of birth into form and our maturation as a human being, most of what we really are remains "unborn." This unborn quality is not something that you lose as you age. It's easy to go into a trance of the mind and believe that you've lost your original state, your true oneness with spirit. But this is just a thought. It is just a trick of the mind. In this very instant, we see this extraordinary form—with blood pumping, heart beating, and lungs breathing. This form has been endowed with the capacity to think and feel and imagine; to love and hate; to question and to assert; and with the amazing capacity to feel sadness, grief, and loss as well as joy, peace, and profound happiness. It almost makes no sense. All of this is part of the expression of your unborn nature, of your spiritual nature. What's unseen presents itself in the form of a body, a mind, and a very unique personality structure. Every birth in the world of physical form is given a sense of self, so that spirit can then operate through it.

TO BE EVERYTHING AND NOTHING AT THE SAME TIME

Is it possible to start to feel, in this very moment, that our bodies, our minds, and even our personalities are ways through which our spiritual essence connects with the world around us? That these bodies and minds are actually sensing organs for spirit? Our physical forms are the vehicle through which spiritual essence gets to experience its own mysterious creation—to be bewildered by its creation, shocked by it, in awe of it, and even confused by it. Spirit is pure potential that contains every possible outcome. From the standpoint of our spiritual essence, nothing is to be avoided. No experiences need to be turned from. Everything, in its way, is a gift—even the painful things. In reality, all of life—every moment, every experience—is an expression of spirit.

Sometimes, we feel clear—free of confusion and indecision. When we're clear about who and what we are, we act in clear ways and respond to life from a place of love, peace, compassion, and understanding. When we're not clear, when we're confused, when we believe things to be true that aren't, how do we act? We tend to act lost, maybe unkind, maybe even cruel. Are there any of us who haven't acted unkind, and then later looked back on it and thought, "Wow! Why did I do that? How could I have done that?" The answer to why you reacted in this manner is true for all of us: it is because you believed something that wasn't true.

When spirit comes into form, it has the potential to become confused, too, and when it does, we experience negative emotions and we act on them. We have to remember that our true spiritual essence isn't just goodness; it isn't just happiness. It's everything and nothing. There isn't a force outside of our spiritual essence. There's nothing but God, as the mystics have told us. Everywhere you look, there's God. Everything you feel, there's God feeling. All of it. We're taught and we're conditioned that God is only the good stuff, that God or spirit or whatever you call it is a "good guy," and all the painful stuff comes from some other source called "the devil" or "evil" or *samsara*. But really, that's just splitting the world up into bits. That's a childish way to understand the divine. If we really want to be awake, if we want to allow suffering to end, we have to open up our very idea of what God is, what spirit is. We have to realize that spirit is an infinite potential that includes everything. And all of our lives are proof that our spiritual nature contains everything at once—that we can become clear or confused, that we can act loving or cruel. How we act and feel depends on how awake we are, and how much we experience that silence, that peace, within.

I remember, years ago, a talk I had with my mother. She was in her fifties at the time. She said, "You know, when I was young, I thought by the time I was fifty I would know everything. I thought I'd be somehow different. But even though I've had a lot of life experience, and there are more things I know now, I'm actually the same as I ever was." At that moment, she was touching upon a very profound truth: there's something about each and every one of us that's the same now as it ever was. You can feel that and sense that right now, in this very moment, because it's that which is aware, right now. It's that which is listening and hearing and feeling, and it's that which is thinking and imagining, right this very moment. Even though you can't conceptualize it, it's there: something you can't quite grasp, but you can never lose. That's what you are: something you can never quite completely imagine, but you can never lose sight of. Everything—your body, my body, everybody's body, everything you see, every piece of dust, every discarded piece of trash on the roadside—is nothing but a manifestation of that pure potential called spirit.

If you look back over your life, isn't there something about you that always remains unchanged? There's something about you now that's the same as it ever was. See if you can feel that. Don't try to understand it. Just feel it. What is it that's there now that has always been there?

THE GREAT RETURN

Jesus once said, "The kingdom of Heaven is spread upon the earth, and men do not see it." We've been given this idea of the kingdom of Heaven, a place of great peace, rest, happiness, and unity. We've been given this idea that we can attain this peace, this rest, in the future, that it's somewhere up in the clouds or in the stars, and that Heaven is some special place, reserved for the very few. But in this saying, Jesus, like so many of the great spiritual masters, reminds us that *this* is Heaven, that everything you see is a manifestation of spirit. Everything is God incarnate. When you open yourself to this, how does it change how you operate in this life? How would you talk to your neighbor if you saw him or her as a very ordinary human being just like you, but also, deep down inside, as the incarnation of God? Could you hold both these realities at once: that all aspects of life have their everyday and normal qualities, but that they are also a complete expression of divinity?

Can you imagine how you might interact with others if you knew they were both at the same time?

Allowing our spiritual essence to come through doesn't mean we must ignore our bodies, minds, and personalities, but we can see that our bodies, minds, and personalities are an expression of spirit. It's not either/or. We can be both body and spirit at the same time, like heads and tails on a coin. What you'll find is that the only thing that can wholeheartedly accept your humanness and this whole, amazing ride of life is your inner spiritual nature. The love that your ego is looking for can only be found in your essence. No "body" and no "thing" can give you enough of it on the outside.

Your inner spiritual presence is an absolute lover of what is, of all of what is. It consciously manifested here, knowing that it was going to be exactly as it is, knowing the danger of this amazing tool of our mind to trick and fool itself. Despite this, it decided to incarnate anyway, taking on this temporary cycle of birth, life, and death, only to realize that its essence has remained the same throughout the whole journey. In the end, there is nothing to be gained or lost. The only possible loss is in closing your eyes to what is.

* * *

Look within, right now, in this very instant. Don't search for anything when you look within. Just look, listen, and feel, and allow yourself to experience that inner presence, that transparency to spirit. You, too, will begin to know what Jesus knew, that you existed before you came into being, and even after you came into being, you still remain, in essence, what you are. To be born simply means that you get to be nothing and something at the same time. Of course we all know that it's easy to lose sight of our divine nothingness when we appear to be something, but the gift of life is that we get to be both simultaneously. This is really our great return. It's a return to our senses. A return to our birth, here and now, to remember who we are. Only then do we get on with the business of how to be what we really are, how to not be lost in our minds. Use your body and mind as an expression of your essence, as a way to connect with others and as a way to remind others of the truth of what we are.

5

Experiencing the Raw Energy of Emotion

ONCE, AT A retreat where I was teaching, a woman came up to the microphone and said, "I feel such immense rage inside me! Even as I'm sitting here at this retreat, where I'm not being disturbed and not being challenged, I just feel so much rage! I look at people, and find myself judging them and being resentful of them for no reason whatsoever. A lot of my life, I've walked around feeling really, really angry."

I could see in her eyes and in the way she held her body that these emotions of rage and anger had really taken over her whole system. What I said was, "I don't want to talk to you. I want to talk to your rage."

At first, she looked at me kind of perplexed. She didn't know what I meant, so I said it again. I said, "I want to speak to the emotion of rage. Tell me how it views life, what it thinks about others. What are its judgments about the most significant people in your life?"

She looked at me with a sense of horror, and she said, "Oh, no! Not that!"

I said, "Yes, yes, yes. That's what I want to talk to. I want you to give rage a voice. Stop holding yourself as separate from it, stop trying to get rid of it. Just for a moment, let your mind become a reflection of it."

Fortunately, she had great courage. Because she had suffered so much, she was willing to take a chance, and so she started to speak to me from the emotion of rage. What spilled out were all of her toxic thoughts and ideas, all the ways her mind had formed conclusions about life and the people in her life, many of which were based on some very difficult moments in her upbringing. As I kept encouraging her by saying, "Yes!" and "Tell me more!" and "Tell me more!" she became more and more willing to let this voice of rage speak. As she did, all of the judgment, blaming, and condemning came out of her. Then, after she spoke in this way for a while, a softer voice began to emerge. It was the voice of deep hurt and sorrow. It was a more intimate, less guarded voice. She was literally giving voice to her pain and suffering. And as she did, I began to see exactly why she was suffering so much.

ALLOW YOUR SUFFERING TO SPEAK

Our suffering consists of two components: a mental component and an emotional component. We usually think of these two aspects as separate, but in fact, when we're in deep states of suffering, we're usually so overwhelmed by the experience of emotion that we forget and become unconscious of the story in our minds that is creating and maintaining it. So one of the most vital steps in addressing our suffering and moving beyond it is first to summon the courage and willingness to truly experience what we're feeling and to no longer try to edit what we feel. In order to really allow ourselves to stay with the depth of our emotions, we must cease judging ourselves for whatever comes up.

I invite you to set some time aside—perhaps a half an hour—to allow yourself simply to feel whatever is there: to let any sensation, feeling, or emotion come up without trying to avoid or "solve" it. Simply let whatever is there arise. Get in touch with the kinesthetic feeling of it, of what these experiences are like when you're not trying to push or explain them away. Just experience the raw energy of the emotion or sensation. You might notice it in your heart or your solar plexus, or in your gut. See if you can identify where the tightness is in your body—not only where the emotion is, but what parts of your body feel rigid. It could be your neck or shoulders or it might be your back. Suffering manifests as emotion—often as deep, painful emotion—and also as tension throughout the body. Suffering also manifests as certain patterns of circular thinking. Once you touch a particular emotion, allow yourself to begin to hear the voice of suffering. To do this, you cannot stand outside the suffering, trying to explain or solve it; you must really sink into the pain, even relax into the suffering so that you can allow the suffering to speak.

Many of us have a great hesitancy to do this, because when suffering speaks, it often has a very shocking voice. It can be quite vicious. This kind of voice is something that most people do not want to believe they have inside them, and yet to move beyond suffering it's vital that we allow ourselves to experience the totality of it. It's important that we open all the emotions and all of the thoughts in order to fully experience what is there.

When you notice some emotional hurt within you, allow your mind to speak to you, inside your head. Or you might even speak out loud. Often I'll suggest to people that they write down what the voice of their suffering says. Try to keep it as short as possible, so that each sentence is contained in and of itself. For example, the voice of suffering might say something like, "I hate the world!" "The world is never fair!" "I never got what I wanted!" "My mother never gave me the love I needed!" and so on. Often, if it's all kept in your head, it just turns into a big muddle. So the first step in releasing this muddle is to speak or write these voices of suffering.

What you're looking for is how your suffering, how the particular emotion you are experiencing, actually views your life, views what happened, and views what's happening now. To do this, you need to get in touch with the story of your suffering. It is through these stories that we maintain our suffering, so we need to speak or write these stories down—even if the stories sound outrageously judgmental or blaming or condemning. If we allow these stories to live underground, in the unconscious mind, all the painful emotions will continue to regenerate.

So now take a moment to allow a piece of your suffering to tell its story. First, name the emotion, then let it speak. What does this emotion think of you? What does it think of others, of your friends, your family? What does it hate most? Why does it appear in any given day? What is underneath these emotions? Let your suffering tell its entire story.

HOW WE MAINTAIN OUR SUFFERING

Recently a woman came to me who was in a deep state of despair. I asked her, "How long has this despair been with you?"

She said, "Almost as long as I can remember."

I asked her, "When did it begin? What age do you remember when this despair really became a very potent and powerful part of your experience?"

She told me this story where she was lying in bed, and she was crying out for her mother, and her mother never came. She kept crying and crying, and still her mother did not come. She told me that she was about six years old at the time. As she lay there, she began to feel like she had been abandoned. This is something that's quite common for young children. When we're very young and we're experiencing anxiety, suffering, sadness, or just confusion, we'll naturally cry out. Oftentimes, if we don't get our emotional needs met, we'll make certain conclusions about life; we'll create little stories in our heads without even knowing it. It might be a story like, "My mother hates me. She doesn't care about me. I never get what I really want." Of course, like all stories, they'll seem very true at the time. When I was talking to this particular woman, her story was that she was abandoned and that she never really got what she needed from her mother.

So I encouraged her to tell the entire story, and when she had finished, I said, "Okay. Now that you've told the story, now that you've gotten in touch with the voice of your suffering, we're going to use the voice of your suffering to free you." And so I asked her to look back and really question the first conclusion that her mind had formed around this event: "I was abandoned when I really needed my mother most." I asked her to keep telling herself that story. I said, "Just in this moment, tell yourself that story, and see how you feel."

She told herself the story, "I was abandoned when I needed my mother most."

I said, "What happens inside you? What do you feel when you tell yourself the story?"

"Despair and sorrow," she said.

And so we went back through it again. "Now tell yourself the story again and again a few more times," I said. I was doing this just so her body and her mind could begin to associate the fact that this conclusion in her mind was maintaining this very potent and powerful experience.

After she told the story a couple of more times, I asked her a question that she didn't expect. I said, "Is this story of what happened really true? Is your conclusion really accurate?"

The first thing she said was, "Yes! I was abandoned, and I needed my mother, and I never really did get what I wanted!"

Once again I asked her, "What happens when you tell yourself this story and you believe it?"

She said, "Well, I feel the despair again. I feel abandonment again. I feel this great, great sadness."

I said, "Well, okay. Remember that event," because we don't want to deny what happened; we're not trying to pretend that what happened didn't happen. I then said, "What I want you to do is to see if you can remember that event, but for just a moment, don't tell yourself any story about it. Don't make any conclusions about your mother, or life, or abandonment, or anything. Just experience it wordlessly."

I could see, as she closed her eyes, she had a memory of what happened. She was going over the memory in her mind; I could see it happening because of the way she held her face and her body. Then she opened her eyes and said, "When I remember what happened, without telling myself a story, without making any conclusion, without blaming or telling myself that I didn't get what I needed, I actually feel better. But you know, my story seems so true! I didn't get what I needed! It did cause me sorrow! I have felt this deep pain ever since!"

I asked her once again, "Experience the same memory, but withhold your story, withhold the conclusions your mind has made. Don't judge yourself for making them; just see if you can experience the story without them." Once again, she closed her eyes and imagined what had happened, and then she opened her eyes, and I said, "Before you tell yourself a story about it, what's the experience now?"

She said, "You know, it's just a memory now. It's just an event that happened, but it's not triggering any feeling in me."

It was at that moment when she began to realize this link between her mind and her body, between her emotional life and her thinking life. She began to see how thought and feeling work together to create suffering; she saw into how this whole phenomenon of suffering works. Almost always, this deep-seated pain and suffering that stays with us for many years, or even throughout an entire lifetime, are held in place by the unconscious conclusions that we make in the moment. These moments might occur when we are young children, or when we come down with an illness, lose our job, or break up with a loved one— any moment where we experience deep sadness, grief, or anger. When you can learn to separate the experience in these moments from the conclusions drawn by the mind, you begin to taste real freedom. You begin to open a space within you where the emotion can come out in such a way that it doesn't have to repeat itself over and over.

HAVING A COMPLETE EXPERIENCE

Painful emotions have a way of regenerating themselves in our systems, moment-by-moment, month-by-month, and year-by-year. If we want to cut this regeneration at its roots, we must come to deeply understand and embody what I call "complete experience." In the face of a difficult emotion, we often turn away from the experience by either repressing it or impulsively acting it out; we do not in fact experience what is there all the way through. We have learned to do this over many years as a way to cope with unpleasant emotions and thoughts as they flow through our lives. Whenever we turn away and avoid what is there, however, we generate future suffering for ourselves and often those around us.

These coping strategies arise in our minds in an attempt to explain the events that happen to us. When we experience painful emotions or feelings, our mind will immediately and sometimes frantically start telling itself a story in order to construct a scenario that will explain why we feel the way we feel. As this process unfolds, we usually go more and more unconscious. By "unconscious," I mean we don't really experience what happened in a completely full and open way. We contract and pull away from the experience, which is actually quite normal. Nobody wants to feel bad, so it seems quite natural to contract and pull away. But anytime we contract from direct experience and spin a story, we have gone unconscious. As soon as we go unconscious, whatever emotion that happened at that time will be locked into our system. It will stay there and regenerate itself over and over again until we find the capacity to experience that emotion without going unconscious in any way.

When I ask people to speak to me from the emotion, it's so that they can begin to hear the story that helped them to go unconscious. Even though our stories about what happened may seem very justified, the important thing to remember is that they actually cause us to go unconscious and lock suffering into our bodies. Instead, what we need to do is to find the capacity to feel what we feel without creating more thoughts about it. When you start to experience a difficult feeling, you see that it's often associated with a memory. As you replay that memory in your mind, if you allow it to be there without a story or conclusion, you start to feel the emotion releasing itself from your system. It may not do this immediately; in fact, for a time the experience of suffering may even intensify. But this is only because you're now experiencing it in a conscious way, not in a numbed or a disassociated way. You're becoming very intimate with the moment-to-moment experience of your suffering.

Our bodies are very well adapted to purge themselves of suffering. When we cry, for example, our bodies are trying to purify us by washing away painful and toxic emotions. But while our body is often trying to help us let go of suffering, our mind is doing the opposite. It's re-traumatizing us with its stories and conclusions. The challenging thing is that whatever conclusions we've made about painful moments in our lives will seem very justified—because our minds are quite intelligent. There will be ample proof for how and why your mind's version of what happened is accurate and real.

Next time you begin to feel some very powerful emotion, see if you can hear the viewpoint that your mind created about it—without judgment, hesitation, or denial. You might need to write it down. Otherwise, it might seem too chaotic. Once you come in contact with the story or view or conclusion which underlies a particular emotion, then you can invite yourself to experience the same thing without the story. Don't worry: the story will be there if you want to go back to it. Through inquiring in this way, your body begins to feel the difference between a raw, pure emotion and an emotion that's old, deep-rooted, and maintained through a story.

LETTING GO OF OUR RESISTANCE TO WHAT IS THERE

Several years ago, I met a gentleman who told me about a painful emotion he was experiencing. I asked him to speak to me from the emotion, to tell me how the emotion felt about him, about the world, and about others. He looked inside, and he said, "You know, Adya, I can't find any story."

I said, "There is one!"

He said, "I really can't find it." So I encouraged him to just be with the emotion over the next week or two, and to come back and share his experience with me. A few weeks later, we talked about his suffering. He told me that he had sat with it for about a week, looking carefully for any story that might be there. At first he was unable to find anything. He then realized, "The reason that I couldn't hear the story of my suffering, that I couldn't hear the viewpoint of my suffering, was because I was keeping myself apart from it. I was merely the witness of it."

I said, "Yes! You have to relinquish the witnessing of it to experience it fully."

What he was able to see was that once he had relinquished the watching of it, the story began to come out, and he just let it flow. Through that process, he saw that it was this combination of feeling and thought that had locked the story in his system, and when he could actually let both out, including the intellectual or thought-based part of the story, the emotion lifted, all by itself.

Another time I met a man in Hawaii who had acquired polio when he was a very young child. He had a condition where certain symptoms of the polio reemerged later in adulthood. He literally wore a cage-like support on his neck and shoulders to hold his head in place, because there was so much pain in his neck, shoulders, and back. He really couldn't function without having his head held up, and he required a massive amount of painkillers just to get through the day.

He told me that one day, when he was in a bookstore, he was reading a book in which he came across the following line: "It's not necessary to resist pain." And he said somehow those words hit him so deeply that he literally dropped the book where he was standing and kneeled on the floor. He was so stunned that he just remained there, unmoving, for about fifteen minutes. He shared with me that this thought—just this idea that it wasn't necessary to struggle against his pain—was so unusual and so powerful that it brought him to his knees.

Like most human beings, it seemed entirely logical to him to struggle against his pain. I'm not talking about emotional pain here, but physical pain—the raw pain that many people live with on a daily basis. While we may be able to free ourselves from suffering, pain is something that is very much a part of human life. No matter how free we become, we'll still be susceptible to pain—to raw, physical pain—from time to time. We can't escape pain, but what we can do is change our relationship with it. What this gentleman told me was that once he got up from the floor of the bookstore, once he recovered from being struck with awe at this one little sentence, he went back home, and over the next few days he noticed he had much, much less pain—about 50 percent less than just the previous day. He went back to his doctor and asked to cut down his pain medication. His doctor suggested that this might not be a wise thing to do, so the man left. He came back a week later and he said, "No. I'm ready to cut down the pain medication. I really am."

Once again, the doctor said, "No, no. I think we should keep it where it is."

Finally he asked the doctor, "Why is it that you don't want me to reduce the pain medicine? I'm telling you that I'm not experiencing the same amount of pain."

Then the doctor asked him, "Are you thinking of killing yourself?"

The man said, "My gosh! No! That's the farthest idea from my mind! I've simply realized that I don't have to struggle against my pain, and this realization has shifted my experience dramatically."

The doctor explained, "Well, sometimes when people who experience a lot of pain say they want to go off their pain medicine, it's because they've made a decision to end their life, and there's a feeling of temporary freedom as a result of this decision. I was afraid that this might be the reason that you wanted to lessen your medication."

The man explained to the doctor that this was definitely not the case; he shared his realization that he no longer needed to struggle against his pain and how due to this realization most of the pain had disappeared. Previously, the way his mind had been struggling with the sensation of pain had made his pain much worse.

I have had an experience very similar to this. Some years ago, I was experiencing pain in my stomach that caused me to seek treatment at a hospital on a number of occasions. On one occasion, I ended up in the emergency room, doubled over in intense pain. I'd never experienced anything like it. My wife asked the nurse if they would give me some painkillers, but they insisted that they couldn't give me anything before I saw a doctor. Like many emergency rooms around the country, it was packed with people, and it took almost three hours for a doctor to see me. As I waited, my pain got worse and worse, and before I knew it I was crumpled up on a seat in the fetal position, literally shaking as my body went into shock. The pain was so intense that my field of vision narrowed, and I felt as if I was going to lose consciousness. To be honest, a part of me hoped I would pass out, because the pain was so intense.

During those hours, I came to a deep understanding, unlike any I had before: It was vital for me to not resist the pain in any way. If I had even a single thought about the future, or about how long the pain might last, or what it might be about, or whether it would ever end, the pain would become even more intense. In response to this understanding, I stayed right with what was happening, without moving into any of the other thoughts that could potentially present themselves. I literally merged with the pain. I won't tell you that it made it go away or that I wasn't in the midst of a great amount of difficulty, but the difference was that I wasn't suffering.

I was in great physical pain, but I wasn't suffering. It was clear to me that suffering and pain are in fact two different things. Suffering is derived from our resistance to what is. This is what causes us psychological, or emotional, suffering. Pain is an inevitable consequence of life. Sometimes we'll experience things that are quite painful. There are some people who live with chronic pain for their entire lives. Having talked to some people who experience chronic pain and who have done some deep introspection, I discovered that the people who deal with pain the best do not believe anything they think about their pain. They do not believe the thoughts they have about the future, and they do not indulge in the mind in trying to rationalize the pain. What they've all told me is that the more involved they allow their minds to be, the more frightened they become and the more intensified the pain.

DROPPING OUR CONCLUSIONS ABOUT THE PAST

When we look directly at that which sustains our suffering, the ideas and conclusions in the mind, it can be quite difficult to let it all go, because in many cases these conclusions appear to be quite reasonable and justified. In fact, it would almost be an insult to suggest that they aren't real. I was speaking with a woman who told me a story about her childhood, and she said, "My mother should have been more kind to me."

I asked her, "Is that really true?"

She looked at me like I was crazy! She said, "Of course it's really true! Parents should treat their children kindly. Everybody knows that!"

I said, "I know that's what we conclude, but is it really true? Is it true that parents should treat their children kindly?" I could see by the look on her face that she couldn't imagine why I was asking this question, because to her it was so obvious. Then I said, "I understand that to treat children kindly is true for you; it's what you value, but obviously it wasn't your parents' truth, because that's not what they did."

When we argue with what was, the only person who is going to suffer is us. It doesn't matter why we're arguing. It doesn't matter how justified our resistance is. When we begin to look deeply at what our mind is doing, we'll see that our conclusions and justifications for our own suffering are what allow the suffering to continue.

It took me a while to work with this particular woman, and I had to invite her to really see that when she tells herself the story, "Parents should treat their children kindly," her body got tighter and more tense, and she felt deeper emotional hurt and even trauma in her heart. My next step was I invited her to have a memory of her parents, but without coming to any conclusions. I could see her thinking and returning to the past, and as she had a memory of some of the things that caused her so much pain, I asked, "What does it feel like when you don't tell yourself anything about the way your parents should have been?"

She said, "Well, it's tolerable. In fact, it feels much better." But then, very quickly, she said, "But it's true! Parents shouldn't treat their children unkindly!"

I said, "Do you really know? Do you actually know that that's really true? We think it's true; we believe it's true; it might be a sacred value for you, but when we impose our present values on the past, we're bound to suffer. The truth is that your parents didn't treat you kindly. That's what's true. That's what happened. They acted in ways that caused you to hurt, and that hurt is real. That feeling is real. That emotion is very real. What you tell yourself about what happened and what people should or shouldn't do, that's never going to be as real as what actually happened."

This is a big leap for a lot of people to make, because we're taught by society, by our schools, by our friends, and by our culture that certain stories and conclusions about life have an objective reality to them. But the truth is that sometimes parents are unkind, and sometimes children are unkind. Sometimes your friends are not kind to you, and I'm sure there have been times when you've not been kind to your friends. You may have experienced some very real suffering, but when we add on top of that what we believe should or shouldn't be, that mental position literally locks the painful emotion into our systems. So even though this is a very difficult thing for people to see because it's so contrary to the way we think, it's absolutely necessary if we're really going to end suffering.

I'm not saying that you should in any way repress what has happened in the past or pretend that it didn't hurt immensely. I'm not asking that people tell themselves the opposite story: "Oh, it's perfectly fine if parents treat their children unkindly." I'm simply inviting you to stay with what has been and what is, now. How do you feel right now? See what it's like when you can feel everything that is there, without telling yourself anything about it. Sometimes the feeling may temporarily get more vivid. It may strike even deeper as the emotion starts to purge itself from your system. As you become more and more conscious, your emotional suffering can become even greater for a short period of time. It's like you're thawing out from a mental and emotional numbness. But this thawing out is absolutely critical. Because unless we purge ourselves of all the stories that contain our suffering, we won't ever feel the freedom and peace of interacting with life from the perspective of truth.

Once you begin to get a feeling for the many ways our thoughts and stories keep us in suffering, you've actually started to tap into something that has a much greater significance. It's something you can use to widen your view of life. Any way that we make a construct out of life, any way that we come to conclusions in our mind about what is or what was or what will be, we are narrowing our experience of life. They are all ways in which we argue with what is. Any time you argue with what was, what is, or what will be, you limit your ability to experience the vastness of who you are. There's no way around it. It doesn't matter what happened, or how cruel someone was, or how unfair something was. It may have been all of those things, and the pain may be very deep and real, but when we have a mental resistance, when we say something should or should not have happened, we're arguing with what did happen or what is happening. When we argue with life, we lose every single time—and suffering wins.

EXPERIENCE THIS MOMENT AS FREE OF SUFFERING

Notice how your body feels when your mind argues with what is. Notice the emotional change happening, and notice what happens when you begin to open your mind just a little bit and invite the possibility—just the possibility—that maybe your conclusions about an event in life, maybe your judgments about it, aren't really as true as you think. Just holding the possibility of that in your mind, you'll see that your emotional environment begins to change. You'll start to come more into the present moment, and this is what freedom from suffering is all about.

When you enter this moment, you begin to experience a moment that is actually free of suffering. If you enter it wordlessly, openheartedly, allowing yourself to feel whatever is there, you find that you've got the key to letting go of suffering right in your pocket. When you start to become present here and now, it's not unusual to feel fear. "Oh! How can I be here and now, that naked, that open? What's going to happen to me? Will I be hurt if I'm fully here and now?" These kinds of questions will come up. These kinds of fears may reveal themselves, and so it does take courage. It does require some willingness to feel what is here, right now. If fear arises, just allow it to arise, and let it purge itself from your body and mind.

In your willingness to pause during a moment of difficulty, to take a few breaths and tune in to all that is there, you may notice that a comforting presence starts to arise. It's by allowing yourself to feel and experience this presence that you can open yourself more and more to what is revealing itself in this moment. Even if it feels frightening, there is an underlying sense of well-being that is always with you and fully available, even if you don't *feel* well. My teacher used to call it "the you who has no difficulty, even when you're having difficulty."

I didn't understand what she was speaking about the first time I heard about this always present "you," but it came to have a great impact on me. It stayed with me, and I thought, "What is that? What is the me that has no difficulty, even when I'm having difficulty?" Because up until that time, I thought either I was having difficulty, or I wasn't. It was one or the other. Yet, when you're experiencing fear, if you really stop and open, you'll see that fear happens within a space of fearlessness, that sorrow happens within a comforting presence, that when we have the willingness to really open ourselves and experience our own resistance to that openness, we experience a state of ease and relaxation that underlies all of our trauma, all of our "dis-ease."

In the end, it's opening to this other field of being—which is literally the foretaste of another state of consciousness—that allows us to move beyond suffering. Suffering is part and parcel of the egoic state of consciousness, where we see ourselves as separate. From that state of consciousness, every painful moment in our life will be interpreted in such a way that it reinforces our sense of separateness and isolation. This is why many people, as they grow older in life, feel more isolated and more separate. So much of life, from the egoic state of consciousness, is easily interpreted as proof that we're actually quite alone, and there really isn't a complete end to suffering, or a true relief from it, when we're confined to these egoic points of view. But by relinquishing our need and desire to control, explain, and believe the way that our minds talk to us about what was and what is, we find a capacity to open to a new state of consciousness.

At first, it's just experienced as a state of stillness, the foretaste of awakened consciousness, where a presence begins to reveal itself. If you allow yourself to relax into this stillness, this silence, you start to witness this presence arise. It may seem like a subtle thing at first, but what's actually happening is that you're beginning to access a whole new state of consciousness—one that is quite immense. By giving your attention to it, by becoming aware of this inner presence and stillness, even in the midst of activity, you make yourself more and more available to the dawning of this vast expanse where you can awaken out of the belief and experience of separation. You realize yourself to be a deep well of awareness—an inner expanse that's always there. You just have to open to it.

Don't try to understand. That will only make it more difficult. Don't think about it. That will take you a million miles away. Just stop and feel it. Stop for a moment, breathe, and begin to notice the you who has no difficulty, the inner presence and stillness, the field of awareness. Every time your mind tries to carry you off by telling its stories of why suffering is justified, you can choose to see that it's not true. You can begin to see that there really is no justified reason why we should be at war with what is. There's no way to win this war. There's no way out of it until we see that it's all imaginary. Very difficult things have happened, and very difficult things may yet happen, but when we encounter them from a state of openness, we realize, bit by bit, that we have a capacity that we never knew was there. We begin to come to know the "you who has no difficulty, even when you're having difficulty." We come to know that there is a great reservoir of well-being even in the midst of incredible grief and loss.

6

Inner Stability

ONE OF THE most important things in life is to be able to find a sense of "inner stability," because it's this foundation that allows us to look into the nature of our experience in a clear and objective way. Unless we can find this inner stability in our lives, we'll always be pushed around by the next experience, by the next thing that happens to us, by the next person or situation that we encounter that is difficult or challenging. Yet, for many of us, a real inner stability—on an emotional and an intellectual level—is very hard to come by.

A helpful analogy for this stability is that it is like the ballast of a boat. Deep in the bottom of every boat is a ballast, which helps prevent the boat from tipping over in the face of the wind. It keeps the boat tracking straight. For a human being, this kind of ballast, or inner stability, comes from our capacity to be open to an interior silence. It's through this inner silence—this inner stillness—that we find a certain stability, so that we're not always pushed around by our minds, by the conditioning that we've all inherited and acquired.

In order to come upon this stability, we have to be able to listen in a new way. It is then that we can experience this deep inner silence. This silence is not merely a quiet mind, where the mind rests and you're not experiencing emotion or feeling, or where you're not hearing or connected with the exterior world. Rather, it's a space within where all our experience naturally occurs. This is a different kind of silence. Usually when we hear about silence, we immediately think of a still mind, a mind that thinks only good thoughts or preferably no thoughts at all. But this is a relative stillness, and all forms of relative stillness are fleeting. Your mind might be still for a short period of time, but then it starts to move again. Your emotions might feel quite balanced and steady in a state of peace for a while, but sooner or later they're going to change.

Every experience—whether inner or outer—changes. The nature of experience itself is change and movement, and this is why so many of us find that we're to one degree or another being knocked off balance and losing our sense of equanimity. The entire world seems to be shifting, and it seems to be happening very, very quickly. So if we're looking for a relative stillness, if we're looking for all of this change and movement to stop, we're always going to be frustrated, because this kind of stillness is elusive, very hard to maintain, and it can slip away in any given moment.

Instead of trying to control our minds or environments by contracting or hiding in order to find this inner stillness, we must throw our senses wide open—listening, feeling, seeing—and become very wide and vast. We welcome all our experience, both that which is happening on the inside as well as that on the outside. When you welcome all of experience into your awareness, a certain type of stillness starts to emerge organically. I'm pointing to a stillness that is directly related to this capacity to open to *all* experiences, not just those that are pleasant and comfortable. Even if you have a very busy mind, if you let go of judging your mind for being busy, even in the midst of the busyness, this stillness is there. Similarly, if you let go of judging the exterior situation—your world—for being noisy or chaotic, even for a moment, this true stillness is there. And when we arrive at this inner stillness and inner stability, our emotional being opens. It is only then that we begin to realize that so much of our instability is caused by our constant arguing with what's happening.

Yet letting things simply be as they are is not something that we're taught. In many ways we're taught to be in a constant state of friction with, to be in battle with what is. We're taught that the way to find happiness or peace is to always be trying to change what is, whether it's changing your inner experience or trying to change the world around you. When we operate from this viewpoint, it puts us in a sense of future, where real freedom or real peace can be found in some time other than now. This leads to our deep-rooted belief that to find peace and freedom, we need to change our inner or outer environment.

To tell ourselves—to tell life—that it shouldn't be the way that it is is a type of insanity. This insanity destabilizes us. It's a bit like going up to a brick wall, telling it that it shouldn't be there, and then continuing to walk into it. Every time you bump your head on it, you judge the brick wall for being there, and then you walk into it again, again bumping your head. Then you say it shouldn't be there, at which point you condemn yourself for the pain you have in your head. It's a kind of insanity to be constantly arguing with what is and thinking it should be different. It's a way that we keep bumping into life. When we collide with life in this way, we always feel interior friction, and we can never find the inner stability for which we yearn.

BEING OPEN MINDED

Before we can really open our senses in order to find our inner stability, we must understand what it means to really open our minds. What does the term "open minded" really mean? We all hear that to be "open minded" is a good thing, yet we tend to turn the idea of open-mindedness into yet another goal we need to accomplish, as if it is some new self-improvement project, something else that we need to achieve.

Open-mindedness comes naturally as we begin to see the ways that we argue with our experience, with events that are in fact immoveable and unchangeable. Of course, the next moment may be very different, and the moment after that may be very different, but this moment is as it is and any moment in the past is as it was. This is a very simple concept, but it's very difficult to let in because it's so contrary to what we've been taught. The conventional worldview involves a constant state of evaluation and judgment. We are even praised for being able to debate and judge. We're constantly saying to ourselves what should and shouldn't be, what we like and what we don't like.

We can open the door and it could be raining, and we might say, "Oh gosh! I hate the rain! It shouldn't be raining! I hate rainy days!" At that moment, we are in opposition with reality. Reality is simply that it is raining; that is what's real. If we argue with it, if we judge it, then we're at odds with life. In many unconscious ways we're taught that if we don't argue with what is, then somehow we aren't doing our jobs as human beings.

But, what is the effect of our constant judgment and evaluation of what was and what is? What effect does this have on us, both individually and collectively? Does it actually lead us to peace? Does it actually lead us to sanity? And most importantly, is it even true? Is it actually true that this moment should be different than it is? Is it actually true that the past should have been different than it was? When we begin to open our minds, we see that this continuous state of evaluation actually leads to suffering. It is when we clearly see this that we can begin to have the capacity to let it go.

When our minds start to open, we're no longer in a constant state of evaluation and judgment. Naturally, then, our senses open—and we can really *see* what is before us. Our eyes open in a different way, our hearing opens in a different way, our emotions open, our hearts open to all of existence. We see how judging and condemning actually close our hearts and harden us to our experience of life and others. Open-mindedness allows you to embrace the nature of your experience. This doesn't mean that you have to like every experience that you have. There are experiences that are painful; there are experiences that are unpleasant. Open-mindedness doesn't mean that you're just opening to the good parts of life; it means you're opening to everything. And this is when you start to discover a type of inner stillness, an inner stability, that vast unchanging expanse that is at the heart of everything.

THE MAGICAL QUALITY OF LIFE

Meeting this stillness, this inner stability, doesn't come from making an effort to be, literally, still. Instead, it comes naturally, on its own, as we open up to life at any particular moment. It's a stillness of inclusion, a kind of stillness that embraces everything. Instead of viewing life as a ground for constant negotiation, you start to see a certain kind of magic inherent in all of existence; there's a mysterious grace that permeates everything. It's not magic because it unfolds in a particular way, however. By "magic," I'm referring to a sense of wonder and deep satisfaction—because life itself is so mysterious. It doesn't unfold according to the way we think it should or even the way we want it to. If we can let go of the way we think it should be, then life starts to reveal its magical qualities.

Essentially, we fall into grace. By that I mean that a certain mysterious quality reveals itself and cradles us within an intimacy with all of existence. This is something that many people are looking for without even knowing it. Almost everybody is looking for intimacy—a closeness, a sense of union with their own existence or with God, or whatever their concept of higher reality is. All this yearning actually comes from our longing for closeness, intimacy, and true union.

When we open to life in this way, we begin to find an inner stability simply because we're no longer at odds with our experience. At any moment we come into an argument with our experience—an argument with life—we can look and see if it actually leads to peace, if it actually makes sense, or if it actually simply leads to discord and conflict. We then begin to find this silence, and we find ground in this silence, which is very stabilizing. There's a sense of homecoming, a sense of "ahhhh, I'm finally in alignment with what's happening." This is the magic. This is what brings forth a sense of inner peace, inner balance, and equanimity. And it is within this silence that true stability is found.

A CONSTANT STATE OF MEDITATION

As we begin to see that the arguments we have with life are a form of insanity, and how egoic consciousness keeps us in suffering, cracks may begin to appear in this old relationship we have with the way we see the world. Our reference for happiness no longer comes from the outside world. It doesn't even come from our inner experience being a particular way; a sense of natural ease and happiness is there simply because we've opened entirely to the way things actually are.

Opening to things as they are is what it really means to be still, to be quiet, to be in a state of meditation. When you no longer resist reality as it is, you could say that you are in a constant state of meditation. We're not just talking about a moment of contemplation or peace, but rather a way of changing our relationship with life such that our experience is not based in conflict, judgment, and constant evaluation. In this way, meditation becomes something that permeates our life in every moment.

This inner stability is so important because without it there's really no clarity. It becomes very hard to clearly see the nature of our experience, the nature of life, and make any sense out of it unless we're looking at it from a perspective of stability, from a sense of stillness. If we have no stillness within ourselves, life can be confusing, threatening, and completely nonsensical. This confusion has nothing to do with life; rather, it has to do with our conflict with life. Conflict isn't inherent in existence. Existence is just the way it is. Conflict only comes from our relationship with life. Inner conflict only comes from our relationship with ourselves.

So it's not so much that we need to change ourselves, but rather it is our relationship with our experience that needs to shift, where our perception of conflict can naturally fall away on its own. It's the only thing that actually opens us to peace, to reality, to seeing clearly. In the end, that's all spiritual freedom is: a simple seeing of self, of life, as it actually is. All we have to do for that to happen is to begin to see that all of the various ways that we argue with existence, although they may seem very reasonable at times, can only lead to suffering and conflict.

But what would happen if we were fully able to be with what is? Many of us wonder, what would happen to the state of the world if everyone just let go and stopped arguing with experience? When we look out into the world, people often say, "My God, the world we've created is very chaotic. There's starvation; there's conflict; there are people in desperate states of suffering all over the planet, and we can't just accept that the way it is. We can't just open and embrace it, because if we do, nothing will ever change for the better." This concern, on the one hand, seems perfectly valid. But what happens when we really ask ourselves, "Does it actually help to stay in conflict with what is? Does it really help the situation to be in resistance with the way things are?" Does it help to be in a constant state of telling ourselves, "This must change! I need to change this!" It seems reasonable that we would want to change that which we perceive as not right, but if our hearts and minds are open, there's an intuitive knowing that no true healing or change can come from this perspective, that this resistance can never bring about the real transformation we're looking for.

I'm not talking about closing our hearts or denying the suffering that's going on in life. Meditation isn't a closing off from life or our surroundings as many people perceive it to be. But what it does involve is a giving up of our resistance to life. There is a difference. And from this constant state of meditation, where we stop resisting, suffering naturally comes to an end, and we discover new and creative ways of addressing the challenges of life.

While we've been looking at approaching the entirety of our life as a kind of meditation, I want to briefly address the topic of meditation as a practice, because it relates to the cultivation of this inner stability that I've been speaking about. The most essential aspect of meditation, what meditation really is or can be, is a relinquishing of control. It can be very helpful to set aside twenty or thirty minutes every day for stillness. You can do this by sitting in formal meditation, by sitting quietly in a room by yourself, or by going for a walk in the woods where you're not talking or engaging the mind. These periods set aside for contemplation can be very powerful, and for most people they are really quite important. They allow us to focus on our experience in a one-pointed way, and they allow us to get glimpses of what happens when we let go of trying to control and judge what arises in our minds.

Meditation, in this sense, is really a state of discovery. Sitting in quiet and stillness and just being in a state of openness gives you a clear opportunity to watch what happens internally when you stop judging your experience, when you stop judging your mind for being busy, or you stop judging yourself for having a particular feeling. You don't try to get rid of the feeling. You don't try to get rid of the mind. You just let go of your judgment. You let go of trying to control the moment. For a while, you surrender into what is.

In these moments of stillness, whether in formal periods of meditation or otherwise, we can begin to let go of our conflict with what is. This is what meditation actually is: letting go of our conflict with life, dropping the struggle with who and what we are. Through resting in this way, we enter a state of nonresistance, where we'll be able to have a taste of what it is like to live for a moment without judgment or conflict. With this as a foundation, it then becomes easier to access these moments of stillness and to let go of the illusion we have of control in our lives.

Especially during challenging times, we are conditioned to move into a conflictual relationship with life, where we habitually evaluate, judge, and try to control particular life situations. If, however, we've had some taste of what it's like to let go, of realizing for ourselves the futility of trying to control things, then we can much more naturally develop a wider perspective on our experiences, even the difficult ones. In this way life itself becomes a meditation, and a whole new relationship with existence starts to unfold.

STILLNESS AS THE ABSENCE OF CONFLICT

From the perspective of ego, it's very frightening to let go and fall into the meditative and still state I'm talking about, because we imagine that doing so would release a sort of chaos—that we'd just sit around all day and do nothing, and that we will no longer be engaged, active participants in life. And we fear that from this stillness, a whole separate kind of conflict will arise. This is the assumption that the ego makes.

If we can set this assumption aside, however, and actually start to investigate what *really* happens when we let go of our resistance to life, we might be surprised by what is revealed. What happens when we stop closing our heart to what's happening and instead open even to the suffering around us? What actually happens when we no longer tell ourselves, "This must change?" The truth, in any given moment, is that things are what they are. If this belief that things truly should be different actually brought about transformative and permanent change in our lives, that would be the end. We'd have our approach. But if we look at what's happening, we come to see that resisting what is there cannot actually change or shift anything permanently. To be in opposition with what is happening, even with suffering, is to continue it.

Opposition, in fact, is its own form of suffering. It is a denial of the stillness that lies within. So when we really look at what happens when we let go of judgment, suffering, conflict, hate, greed; when we stop judging it and saying it should or shouldn't be there, what happens inside of us? Do we close off, shut down, and turn from life? Is that actually what happens when we embrace life as it is? I would suggest that something else happens, something quite different from what the ego would expect. What actually happens when we stop judging, when we stop resisting the flow of our lives, is that we come into an alignment where we are in a natural and clear relationship with whatever presents itself.

From this place of alignment, the perspective we come upon is not the perspective that we anticipate. It's not the fearful place of the ego. The ego thinks we would become indifferent to everything and uncaring in the face of this nonresistance. But actually something different happens. Instead of being uncaring, we actually come into a deeper and more intimate relationship with what's happening. We become very deeply connected. We find ourselves able, in the moment of someone's actual pain or in the middle of our own suffering, to connect very intimately, very purely, without any resistance. This opens up a door within us for an entirely different response—a response that's not based in opposition. Instead, this intimacy and stillness guides us into a very precise and effective type of action, a kind of involvement born out of a deep inner connection with life and with others. This response is not based in conflict, but in wholeness and oneness. When we're not responding out of conflict, division, and resistance, what manifests is pure compassionate action, wise action that comes from intimacy, stillness, and true connection.

In stillness, the various aspects of one's spiritual unfolding come together, because it's from the state of stillness, of nonconflict, that our deeper unfolding happens. This space is a natural stillness—natural in the sense that we're not *trying* to be still. We simply realize that the only thing that can keep us from being still is when we argue with what is, when we judge or condemn what is or what was or what might be. This is the only way that we can create chaos. Inner stillness is nothing but the absence of conflict.

The greatest generator of conflict, both internal and external, is our addiction to interpreting and evaluating each and every moment of our experience. When we continually judge and evaluate, we separate from what's happening. We feel a certain distance from our experience, because now we have become the evaluator of the moment and we're no longer in unity with the flow of existence and of life. We then find ourselves acting like a sports commentator to our own lives—making comments without actually being in the game. When we judge, we move to the sidelines of our own existence.

This phenomena of our urge for constant commentary in order to step outside of actual experience is evidenced in the many cable news programs in which there's really very little "news" offered but rather a forum for constant interpretation, evaluation, and judgment. The idea seems to be that if we can pit two sides against each other, arguing and debating their points of view, somehow we're going to arrive at a larger or more complete sense of the truth. It doesn't usually happen this way, though. Instead, everything usually devolves into more conflict, less clarity, and more solidified belief systems. The "truth" that was sought after becomes just another set of conditioned thoughts, beliefs, and opinions.

This dynamic happens even in the most casual of conversations. Look carefully at your own dialogues with others, and in the dialogues of those around you, and you can see the many ways we evaluate and interpret the people and the events in our lives. In this way, we are just like the pundits on television, moving further and further away from stillness and closer and closer to conflict, with the predictable outcome of more tension and less reality.

A DIFFERENT DIMENSION OF BEING

As we begin to meet life as it is rather than as we think it should be, as we let go of our need to control and continuously interpret our experience, we start to open to life in a completely new way. We become deeply grounded in silence. The nature of this silence is a lack of conflict with life, and the more we open to this state of nonconflict, to this state of inner stillness, we begin to fall into the grace of a different dimension of being—a dimension rooted in a deep intimacy with our own lives and with existence itself.

As I noted earlier, part of moving into this new dimension of being often involves the appearance of certain cracks within the framework of our habitual way of perceiving life. We start to become aware of a bright light that is able to shine through these cracks and into our experience. Magic and mystery reveal themselves as our old conditioned view of reality breaks apart, and something completely fresh and different comes in. It is as if this new way of looking at things has always been there, but we weren't ever quite able to access it. This newfound perception is grace, where we receive and experience something that arrives from beyond the way we normally perceive life.

Through this grace we are actually drawn more and more into this new dimension, this new way of perception. From the standpoint of ego, during these very transformative and illuminating experiences, we feel hesitant or even afraid, because the conceptual world with which we've walled ourselves in is starting to break down. Though limiting and quite frustrating, these habitual ways of seeing the world are familiar; they've been a home to us. We know intuitively that we have begun the process of going beyond the way we viewed life in the past. It's like waking up from a dream. All of a sudden we wake up to the fact that the entire way we viewed our lives was just a very thin veil that obscured the greater reality.

This other dimension of existence is extraordinarily rich and full of meaning—not meaning we can describe or understand it with the mind, but with a felt sense of a great vastness and value, something of profound significance. These tastes of a new dimension are moments of grace— and these moments pull us deeper and deeper into reality itself, into a perception where we know in the core of our hearts that everything really is one in essence, that there really is that which connects us all as a single whole.

From our conceptual world view, oneness is simply an idea, but once we begin to be pulled into this new way of being, oneness is no longer just a concept built on thought. Rather, it's an actual lived experience of a tremendous intimacy with each and every aspect of our lives. Even the most mundane and ordinary objects in our lives—events and people and circumstances—become transparent to this inner connectivity. What's actually happening is that we're beginning to see the face of the divine in each and every moment of our lives.

So just what is this new dimension of being? Can we just peek through and experience this moment as it truly is? Can we experience this grace right now, at this very moment? Allow yourself to experience life outside the old shell of separation. Look at the most ordinary thing; any-thing will do. How does it look? How does it feel? What is the sense of it when you don't name it, when you don't say it's beautiful or ugly or right or wrong? What's the actual experience of anything beyond the veil of separation? If you're very, very quiet and you open your senses all at once, you just might be taken. You might be taken by a moment of grace and fall into a sense of what it really feels like when life is not separate from you, when life is not other than you, when life is actually an expression of something indefinable, mysterious, and immense.

7

Intimacy and Availability

"NOT KNOWING" IS something that is undervalued in our culture. Most of us are conditioned to believe that not knowing isn't a very worthy trait. When you take a test at school, for example, and you don't know the answer, you feel anxious, like you've done something wrong, and you feel stress as you try to remember and you try to know. But in the context of spiritual inquiry, we actually let go of trying to know. We let go of conceptual certainty.

Right now, you can allow yourself to experience a very simple sense of not knowing—not knowing what or who you are, not knowing what this moment is, not knowing anything. If you give yourself this gift of not knowing and you follow it, a vast spaciousness and a mysterious openness dawns within you. Relaxing into not knowing is almost like surrendering into a big, comfortable chair; you just fall into a field of possibility.

When you first encounter this field of not knowing, you may feel vulnerable; this field of uncertainty may make you feel naked, as though you are unable to protect yourself. You can inquire directly into this: What is the you that feels vulnerable? What is it, really? Your mind will tell you that this you who feels vulnerable is actually something real, something that actually exists. But if you look at it, what you'll begin to see is that it's just a thought: "I'm vulnerable." It's a thought based on memory. Every one of us, through the process of growing up, has had moments when we've felt very open and exposed, where someone has come in and taken advantage of us, lashed out against us, or told us we were wrong. We learned that being wide open may not be the best idea.

Most adults are desensitized to the openness and the innocence of a child. When as children our natural vulnerability is violated, an imprint is left, a memory of hurt, which results in a recoiling. These kinds of memories often remain with us, causing us to conclude: "If I allow myself to be too open, too vulnerable, I'm likely to get hurt. I really shouldn't do this." However, vulnerability is always there, whether we're consciously opening to it or not. It's not like we're more protected when we armor ourselves with self-image and other ideas about who and what we are. In reality, the effort of armoring ourselves really doesn't work.

When we armor ourselves, when we close from natural openness and vulnerability, what is it that we're protecting? Are we protecting something that's actually here, or are we merely protecting an idea of ourselves, held in memory? If the feeling of openness and vulnerability triggers a memory in the present moment, just allow that memory, along with all its associated emotions, to arise. But see it and feel it for what it is: a memory reemerging in the current time, in the space of right now. If you know it's just a memory that got triggered from this space of openness, then you realize it's not something that's happening now. Rather, it's the arising of the past. Now it's not so intimidating, it's not so threatening. It's okay if old memories arise; they're not problems in and of themselves.

PURE INTIMACY AND THE OPEN EXPANSE OF BEING

As you get accustomed to relaxing more and more into the space of not knowing, you'll notice a growing sense of becoming intimate with yourself, even though you don't know what you're intimate with. We usually think of intimacy in terms of "what *I* am intimate *with.*" This view assumes a separation between the "I" and "what I'm intimate with." This isn't the kind of intimacy that arises in the openness of not knowing. What arises in this openness is *pure* intimacy. It's not a closeness with one thing or another. It's a feeling of absolute union with every part of experience, with life itself.

There was a great Zen master named Dogen who lived hundreds of years ago, and one of his definitions of enlightenment was "intimacy with the ten thousand things." Of course, in the context of his teaching, the "ten thousand things" refers to everything. So when we open to this space of unknowing, we start to feel a literal intimacy with every part of our experience. The sense of distance starts to drop away, and arising within that field of unknowing is a sense of presence. It's a very subtle thing. We begin to touch upon something without boundaries, without walls, without definitions, without borders. We're touching upon something that's immensely vast.

One of the primary qualities of this space of unknowing is that it is aware; there's a completely natural awareness or consciousness flooding the whole of experience. Awareness simply means that there is a pure perception of whatever you're experiencing. The unknowing is itself aware, is itself conscious. The Tibetan Buddhists call this "self-luminosity." The deepest reality of who we are is this open field of awareness that is self-luminous, self-knowing. In other words, who and what we truly are knows itself. It knows itself as a field of unknowing, as an open expanse of being. It's not an unconscious expanse of being; it's a knowing expanse.

By allowing yourself to viscerally and emotionally connect with this open expanse of being, it's possible that you will see that this open space of unknowing, this pure field of awareness, is actually what you are at the most essential level. It's the part of you that has always existed and that never changes. Everything that occurs comes to be within this field of awareness and pure being. If you allow yourself to feel it, to sense it, you'll see that this deep field of unknowing has been with you all along, that there's literally not any moment, ever in your life, where it was absent.

THE ALIVE FIELD OF UNKNOWING

Though it is hard to grasp, it's important to realize that this inner state of not knowing is not a dead or inert place.

Sometimes when I describe it people reasonably interpret what I'm saying to mean that the goal is to not know anything. I'm not actually saying, "Never know anything." That would be nonsensical. There are many things in life that are very helpful to know: We need to remember our name, we need to know where we put our car keys, we need to know all sorts of information so we can go about our day and accomplish our tasks. It's not this sort of relative, practical knowing that is a problem or that needs to be forgotten. This sort of knowing is not in opposition to this greater field of unknowing; it's what arises within it, whatever you need to know whenever you need to know it.

This practical knowing is in no way diminished by opening to this deep well of unknowing. What arises from this core of our being, however, is a whole different type of knowing, not the kind of knowing that the mind creates itself around, or that turns into the endless stream of belief, ideas, opinions, and points of view. This new way of knowing is what we refer to when we speak of an "insight" or an intuitive understanding. This clear seeing then allows for a new way of relating with and using the mind, which I call "inspired thinking."

Inspired thinking arises out of interior awareness. From this silent expanse, you gain access to a new kind of thought. Inspired thinking is literally an expression of the unknown. You cannot control it; you cannot will it to do one thing or another. Most of us very rarely experience inspired thinking; it's not something that we experience day to day. But it is possible to experience this kind of thinking more and more frequently, until it becomes the normal way that we move through life.

LIFE DEMANDS A RESPONSE

None of us ever knows what's going to happen from one moment to the next. We never know what's going to be demanded of us in any given moment. We really don't know anything other than this moment, right here, right now. But one thing we can be fairly certain of is that the next moment is going to be a little bit different than this moment, that life undulates and moves and is very unpredictable. Like an ocean, sometimes in life the waves are calm and easy, while at other times they're rough and challenging.

Because the nature of life is uncertain and changing, not subject to our own needs for predictability and control, we can't imagine how we could actually live from this deep space of awareness. Our minds can't imagine living life in a way that is this open and groundless. What often happens is that we'll begin to touch this deeper ground of being and then something happens, and we get pulled out of it. The kids are crying. You have to go to work. Someone calls you on the phone and it's an emergency. You find that a friend or co-worker is agitated and you get lured into an argument. If we lose our awareness in these types of situations, if we become unconscious, then we get pulled from the ground of being. We tend to go right up into our minds, and we start to relate to the world from the standpoint of thinking. Life can be very challenging and it therefore demands something from each of us. It demands a response.

I want to introduce a phrase, said by an old Zen master, which I really like. He called this space of not knowing "doing nothing." In this space, there's "no doing happening," which means we're not leaping back into the mind and starting to do—creating beliefs, ideas, and opinions. To clarify, he emphasized the word "doing," rather than the word "nothing," to make a point that there is a way that this field of being can actually manifest as action, as doing. Doing nothing does not refer to just sitting in a cave all day or on the couch avoiding what is happening in our lives. But it *is* pointing to a very fresh and creative way of responding to our lives, to the spontaneous action that arises directly from the reality of not-knowing.

So how do we begin to respond to life from this state of unknowing? How do we respond without going back into the matrix of the mind? How do we respond without being caught, once again, in old habits of action and reaction? That is a very deep question: How do we "do" the doing of nothing? How do we *be,* as a verb, the depth of our being?

WISE ACTION AND A NATURAL RELATIONSHIP WITH THOUGHT

Most of our greatest challenges as human beings take place within the arena of relationship. When I speak on this topic, I'm referring to *all* of relationship, to the entirety of relationship. The most primary relationship is the one that each of us has with this moment. What is the nature of the relationship that we as this deep well of unknowing awareness have with this moment? It is simply allowing this moment to be as it is; it is the space that allows whatever arises in this moment to be that which it is. In fact, this is exactly why everything that happens simply happens as it does, because the depth of being allows it to do so—not because our awareness chooses to allow it to happen, but because there is literally no other option.

The reason for this is very simple: this pure awareness that we are is not separate from anything that happens. Everything and anything we can possibly imagine—including all the images in the mind, all our thoughts, all our experiences, and all the various ways that humans can create suffering—arise from that deep well of unknowing awareness; in fact, everything is an expression of it. In other words, there's no separation between the ground of being and the myriad expressions arising out of it. From the perspective of the ground of being, its relationship with this moment is such that it can never change, alter, or manipulate that which is.

That would be great and wonderful if just accepting the moment as is, without doing anything, was the end of the story, but as everybody knows, it's not quite this simple. We also need to respond to each moment, to act; that's part of relationship, too. We find ourselves having to respond—to the environment, to the events and situations around us, and to other human beings. This is actually where the rubber really hits the road. This is where we can most clearly see how deep our experience of this ground truly is. How thoroughly have we returned to stillness? What we come to see is that there is nothing quite like our day-to-day relationships to show us where we really are, to show us firsthand our level of realization.

So after we've looked at this fundamental relationship we all have with this moment, we begin to work our way out. As we've seen, there are times when it is very helpful to think, and to think clearly. The truth is that we don't really have a lot of control over what we think. Thoughts occur whether we want them to or not. Obviously, we have to think. There are many, many moments when we have to use our mind—especially when we engage with others. The question becomes: What is the correct, or most natural, relationship with thought?

Out of this ground of being, what we've seen is that we can't actually look to thoughts to tell us what's ultimately true and real. In this deeper awareness, the way that we use thought and language becomes much more fluid, because we don't have to protect our thoughts. We no longer have to assert our beliefs, which are merely thoughts, in a domineering manner. In other words, the way we speak the thoughts that arise in our mind, and the way we communicate, are done from a much lighter place, because we know that reality is something that arises from beyond thinking. In this way, thinking becomes a way to express ourselves, not a means to demand that reality be the way we think it should be.

Thought, language, and communication—these are all beautiful ways of expressing ourselves, our deep nature, our creativity, and our intelligence and our wisdom. When we're truly able to know that whatever we think or say isn't the ultimate truth, then communicating becomes much more of a dance, a play, because we don't have to win or end up being right or correct in our communications. When we realize that what we think and say isn't ultimately the truth, then what we think and say can always adapt itself to the moment. This, in fact, is what "wise action" is: Activity, speech, and relationship that arises from wisdom and is in harmony with the moment. It is action that changes and molds itself to each and every moment. Each and every moment requires a different response than the last moment. Each conversation requires that you say something different than you did in the last communication.

Wise action is in fact what I am practicing here. I'm using concepts, ideas, and thoughts to express something that's beyond them, to give voice to something that transcends them. As long as I realize that what I'm trying to communicate is actually beyond the words, and is the space from which the words derive their inspiration, then my thoughts and words have a lightness to them. Thus, the way I communicate is more transparent, which means my words and ideas here are open to the response of somebody else reading them. Ultimately, when we imbue our communication with wise action, we will tend to be understood more clearly by those with whom we are in relationship.

Relating and communicating in this transparent way may sound like something simple. In many ways it sounds so much easier to not get caught in our ideas or to refrain from using them to defend, or to argue, or to convince someone of something. What most of us experience, however, at least in the beginning of this exploration, is that it's not all that easy. The truth is that most of us are not accustomed to using communication in this light and open way. Rather, we're actually way too identified with our thoughts, beliefs, and opinions to be light and easy. Are we willing and able to have them change, at a moment's notice, if the situation dictates it?

In order to gain this degree of lightness and ease in the way we relate to others, we must deeply examine and meditate upon the true nature of thought, of our relationship with it. We must clearly see the ways that we're deceived by the thinking process, and how in fact we use thought to deceive others in the process of convincing them that our beliefs and opinions are actually real.

STAYING IN BEGINNER'S MIND

How do we communicate from a place of ease, from a place that's undefended and unguarded, in a way where we're willing to change as our views change? It may make sense in theory—but is it even possible in real life? Are we really willing to be wrong? How do we stay open and innocent, in the moment, to reality as it presents itself to us?

My teacher used to say, "Stay in beginner's mind. Never leave beginner's mind," because in beginner's mind, the possibilities are infinite. They're open. Anything can happen. You're open to learn anything you need to learn. If your view of something needs to change, you're open for it to change. No matter how deeply you've seen something, no matter how much you *think* you know something, stay in beginner's mind. Don't get rigid. No matter how great a revelation you may have had, no matter how great an opening in the core and depth of your being, if you stay in innocence, in the mind that's very light, that never takes its ideas as truth, then there will be a much greater potential for your thoughts, as well as your communications with others, to be naturally inspired.

We've all had experiences where others have used their words as weapons against us. Beginning in very early childhood, our parents, at times, would get angry, upset, or frustrated and say something that was quite hurtful. Many people have deeply ingrained memories of being emotionally wounded by the way someone spoke to them. It's not only important that we speak from a place that is not hurtful to others, but also that we learn how to listen from this deep well of being, from this expanse of vast awareness and unknowing, from the beginner's mind.

For a moment, you might inquire: Are we actually ever listening? This is another one of those questions that seems very simple, but it's actually quite deep: Are we actually listening? How often do we actually listen to each other? If we observe, what we often see when two or more people are communicating with one another is that the one who is not speaking is simply waiting for a gap in the conversation so they can once again assert what they think. But if we're going to communicate from an inspired place, from a place of inner peace and beginner's mind, then we won't use our words and our language as weapons. Even if others speak to us in this way, it is possible to not be pulled into the trance of their words. When we come to see that words aren't the truth, that what people say about us tells us about *them,* not us, we don't worry so much about what someone might say about us. And when you say something about someone else, you can actually see that in most cases you're revealing more about yourself than about the other, revealing your projections and your ideas.

TRUE HUMAN INTIMACY

In order to deeply connect with others, we must find a way to make ourselves fully available. By "available" I mean an openness to real, true intimacy. Most people will say that they like intimacy, they like closeness, but it's quite rare to find somebody who really wants to be intimate. I'm not just speaking about physical intimacy. I'm talking about a psychological intimacy, a spiritual intimacy, an emotional intimacy, because there is no intimacy without true availability. When we become intimate with another human being—a lover, a friend, or even a stranger we're simply conversing with—and we actually *open* ourselves in an undefended way to the other person, we're doing something that human beings rarely do.

We tend to be quite protective, holding ourselves back behind some wall of fear, usually a fear of the very thing that we crave—closeness, intimacy, and union. Why is it that we crave these things? Because, in reality, the fact is that we are actually one; we are all intimately connected. Therefore, we are all naturally pulled to this union and intimacy, though we are also simultaneously frightened by it. As a result of painful experiences from childhood, where we made ourselves so open and vulnerable and suffered as a result, there are very strong memories or stories we carry with us that keep us in fear. Somehow, we must find the willingness and the courage to open ourselves to true relationship, so that we can become once again open to true intimacy. Whether through a relationship with another human being, with the environment, or even simply with our own self, the invitation is to come into this true intimacy, this profound sense of human connection.

Very few human beings can be truly intimate with themselves, as most have never really looked deeply into the truth of who and what they are. So when they experience themselves alone—sitting in a room or waiting for a bus—there's a nervousness or an anxiety that arises. If all we know of ourselves is a collection of thinking, memory, and identification, there will always be some sense of agitation. This is why most human beings have a difficult time being alone: because when they're left alone, they're left with their thoughts, they're left with their images and ideas which, for many, are quite torturous.

So, again, we have to start with a willingness to enter into ourselves, to be alone for a moment and enter into what we really are. It is then that we have the capacity to open to each other—to be available, intimate, and connected. We have to be willing to face any fear that might arise in our experience.

As a spiritual teacher I've seen over and over again that people can have very deep and powerful spiritual revelations, even real awakenings to the truth of their nature, and yet at the same time they can still have a deep hesitation or even fear to enter into real human intimacy.

Intimacy with reality is one thing. Actually, intimacy with reality is relatively easy, once you get the hang of it. Once you get the hang of being with yourself, being with your own unknowingness, you realize that it's not really difficult, after all. It's a process of relaxation, not a process of struggle. But to be very open and intimate with another human being, that's not so easy, at least initially. To do so requires a depth of insight and a deep willingness to open to fear—to be willing to see those parts of you that don't want to open. Further, we must come face to face with the whole world of emotion—emotional protection and emotional availability. Through relationship, we can start to see how we often go into a mode of self-protection or recoil, or into various degrees of fear. While much of this resistance is fueled by thought, this whole arena of intimacy and availability is something that also takes place on a deeply emotional level. To be open-minded, to be no-minded, is one thing, but to be genuinely emotionally open is something deeper, and it touches the heart and core of us in a very profound way. It requires that we stay in beginner's mind and, more importantly, in beginner's heart.

BEING INTIMATE WITH FEAR

I'd like to tell you that there's some easy, two- or three-step process that will guarantee emotional openness and availability whenever you want it, but it doesn't quite work that way. Even though we'd all like accessing this openness to be that simple, we know, from our own experience, that this is rarely the case. The most important thing when it comes to emotional openness and vulnerability is a willingness to face our fears, because many of our fears, although they're created in the mind and memory, are also deeply lodged into our emotional makeup. They can't just be swept away as if we're sweeping dust off the sidewalk with a broom. There has to be a willingness to feel that fear again, feel the hesitation, feel the tendency to recoil—if it's there—and to have the willingness to move into it, to actually become intimate with the fear itself. Union with fear isn't something that many of us consider when we think of intimacy and relationship. But when you are willing to be intimate with your resistance, closer than you imagine, then you will see that your fears are not your enemies; they are your allies.

Most people have experienced fear in their life, and I often hear people say, "Well, I know I'm intimate with fear because I feel it so profoundly." Some people, when they begin to become intimate with another human being, become profoundly fearful. Deep terror can arise. In this case, someone might say, "Well, I'm terrified! Of course I'm intimate with it!" But you can actually experience a deep level of emotional pain, turmoil, and fear even without being completely available and intimate with these experiences. So then what does it mean to be intimate with fear, with anxiety, with some of these emotional barriers that hinder one's direct experience of oneness? What does it mean to be intimate with the moment of fear?

Sometimes, as in this case, it's best that you live with a question rather than search for an answer. What is it like to be intimate with fear? It's the same as being intimate with a view of a sunset, or the leaf on a tree, or the smile in a child's eyes. It's different emotional content, of course—it may be much more intimidating—but really what it means to be intimate with fear is the same as what it means to be intimate with anything else: Instead of running away from it, trying to solve it, making it into your problem, you can actually get very close to it. "Getting close" doesn't mean you snuggle up to it. Getting close simply means you stop running away. You don't have to run toward it. You just have to stop running away. Then you'll feel an intimacy. You may also feel a resistance, but you can choose to stay right there.

Of course you don't like it. Of course you recoil. That's what you're taught to do. That's what our whole society told you that you needed to do. Even part of your brain has evolved such that when you experience fear, you feel compelled to flee. If you're out in the jungle and you feel fear because some animal is about to attack you, it's wise that you feel this desire to run away quickly. It's good that you don't sit there with a willingness to feel intimate with your fear, because you might get caught and killed. But the truth is we're not in the jungle, and usually, when we experience fear, especially the fear of being open and intimate, that kind of fear isn't the same as the fear you have in the jungle. Interestingly, it feels the same, but the response that's called for is something entirely different. When you remind yourself that what you're dealing with is fear within your own mind, you see that it's a completely different kind of fear. It's a fear that's created within your own being, and you can't outrun yourself. You can't run so far, so fast that you get even one inch away from yourself. There's no possibility of running from yourself. There's no hope that you will be able to escape yourself.

All of us feel—in the depth of our being we know—it's not just good enough to feel open and free and at peace when we're left alone or when our environment is very supportive. These things are beautiful, and can show us the possibility of freedom, but at an even deeper level we're all called to express this freedom, openness, and intimacy within the context of relationship.

Ultimately, we're going to have to open our heart to the whole world, to everything that's happening in it, and to everything that has ever happened. We're going to have to open our heart to everything that could possibly happen. Why? Because we're not separate from anything or anyone. Anything you consider separate from you can scare and can intimidate you. But when you have the willingness to open your heart, to be intimate even with the things you don't like, with the people and events that frighten you, with the state of the world that may intimidate you, then you'll find a way in which the core of you has an avenue through which to express itself. You can express and manifest the very depth of yourself in the outside world, so that there's no longer a division between inside and outside and there's no longer a boundary for our love.

WHAT REALLY WANTS TO BE EXPRESSED?

I want to share a story from my past that will help illuminate what I mean by this deep intimacy when it comes to a moment of relationship. When I was nine or ten years old, I got in trouble for something that happened one day, and my mother sent me to my room and said, "Wait for your father to get home." About an hour later, my father came home from work. Apparently what I had done was pretty stupid. My father entered the room and, like some parents in that generation, he gave me a little spanking. He never spanked me very hard, just enough to let me know I'd really done something wrong. He then left the room, and I was alone.

About five minutes later, he came back in, sat down next to me, and said, "You know, I really hate this. I really hate coming in here and having to spank you. I'm not going to do that ever again. I just hate doing that." And he also said, "And I hate coming home from work and finding out that the first thing I have to do is discipline you. That's really a hard thing for me. Let's just not do this anymore, okay?"

I looked at him, and we gave each other a big hug. That moment touched me so deeply. I had done something wrong, and he was supposed to go in there and give me a spanking, and that's what he did. But after he left, he was able to be intimate with what he *really* felt underneath. Of course, when he came home from work, he wanted to hug me and tell me he was glad to see me. Instead, having to spank me caused him to connect deeply with this disappointment and the suffering around it. There was something about him walking back in my room and being that honest, that intimate, and that willing to share something about himself which completely transformed our relationship.

In our own ways, neither my father nor I wanted to feel like this again, and so we agreed that we weren't going to go through that interaction again in the future. Connecting in this way brought us to a very close and intimate place. He stopped being a parent for that moment, and in some ways I stopped being a child. I grew up enough in that moment to meet him, hear what he was saying, and see things from his point of view. I realized that it hurt him to discipline me in this way, and he wasn't going to do that anymore. This was a very simple exchange, but to me it was a very profound moment of real intimacy with my father, in which he was very open with me. And in this openness our whole relationship was able to shift.

I'd like to share another story with you, one where I was the one who opened to a certain intimacy and expressed it. Not too long ago I was in my office, and I was talking to a woman who had worked there for a long time; she helps with some of the materials that we produce. She was working on the newsletter, which I was reviewing. After I'd checked in and given my okay for certain things, we just naturally entered into a casual discussion. She started to tell me about her experience, about how she felt somewhat unappreciated for what she did. I let her talk and share her experience with me.

After she finished talking, I sat there for a moment in quietness, and I realized I was kind of confused, because I was thinking, "Wow. My memory is that I've given a lot of acknowledgment and a lot of praise for the work that she had done," so I felt perplexed about her not feeling acknowledged. I then began to try to explain what I was feeling, what I was observing, and right in the middle of the first sentence that came out of my mouth, I just stopped. What I realized is that she didn't actually need me to tell her that I appreciated what she'd done. I'd done that probably hundreds of times, and even though that's what she was saying she wanted, I realized that's not really what she needed. Beneath the surface of what she was saying, she wanted something much deeper. So instead, I found this coming out of my mouth, "What I really want to say is not that I appreciate you, but that I really love you. I really love who you are and what you are, and not just what you do."

As soon as I said those words, tears started to come out of her eyes, and I realized that's what she'd needed to hear. When I'd stopped in the middle of starting to explain myself, in that moment when I stopped, there was an instantaneous meeting inside of true intimacy and true availability. When I stopped, I realized what she needed to hear, what she really wanted to hear, what she wanted to know. I also realized what was really true: that I did love her. I love everybody in that office. I don't just like them and appreciate them, but there's a really deep love and bond. As soon as she heard that, it shifted something. It shifted something for her, and it shifted something for me.

These are little examples of moments where it could have so easily gone a different way. My father could have so easily not come back into that room and told me what he was feeling. I could have so easily said, "Wow! What I remember is me telling you that I appreciated you at least a hundred times." I could have said that, and that would have even had some truth to it, but that wasn't the truth of the moment. It wasn't the truth of what needed and wanted to be expressed. In both of these cases, there was a willingness—first on my father's part, and then on my part—to stop and feel what really wanted to be expressed. When we stop in this way, we come into a deep intimacy with our own experience, and we become deeply intimate with what really wants to be communicated. We connect not just with what *needs* to be communicated, but with what really wants to be said from the deepest level and from a very unprotected place.

8

The End
of Suffering

THERE'S ONE THING about which I would like to be completely clear: If we want to stop suffering, if we really want to bring an end to suffering, we've got to wake up. "Waking up" means awakening to the truth of our being, and it also means waking up from a whole host of illusions.

The truth is that waking up can be a disturbing process. Who really wants to find out that everything they thought was real was nothing but a pocket full of dreams? Who wants to find out that everything they hold onto and cling to *is* the very reason that they suffer? Who really wants to find out that we're all addicted to qualities like approval, recognition, control, and power, and that none of these things actually brings an end to suffering? In fact, they're the cause of suffering! So the truth is that most of us don't really want to wake up. We don't really want to end suffering. What we really want to do is *manage* our suffering, to have a little bit less of it, so that we can just go on with our lives as they are, unchanged, the way we want to live them, maybe feeling a little better about them.

But there is a disturbing truth here. The disturbing truth is that coming to the end of suffering isn't really a personal matter at all. Coming to the end of suffering has to do with reality and truth, with what's real as opposed to what's not real, and valuing what's actual instead of what's imagined. The whole process of awakening from the dream is very profound, and for most people there's a real difficulty and even a disturbing quality to it because it means we have to look at ourselves in the mirror. I don't mean looking at ourselves in the mirror the way we usually do—with regret, judgment, and blame. I mean looking in the mirror in a different way, where we're finally willing to see we are the ones who are causing our suffering, and it's we alone who can find the way out.

So waking up is a bit like what an alcoholic or a drug addict experiences when they are coming out of their addiction. Most addicts only let go of their addiction when they've really seen that there's no possibility of being happy *and* being an addict. Up until that time, most addicts are in a constant process of negotiation with life. They think, "Well, I can be an addict some of the time," or, "I can be a little bit of an addict, but not a lot of an addict," or, "I can quit whenever I really want to." They try to moderate their urges—but in between it all, their urges still have the upper hand and spiral them into suffering. So when does an addict actually stop? They tend to quit when they hit bottom, when they've seen the wisdom of absolutely no escape, that nothing's going to work except facing themselves and their situation where they are.

For a lot of us, we can look at others who seem to be struggling and say, "Well, at least I'm not an addict. I'm not an alcoholic. I don't abuse drugs." But truthfully almost all of us are addicts and the deepest thing we're addicted to, our drug of choice, is actually suffering. The very thing we want to be without is the thing we're addicted to, and that's suffering. Not many people will admit it. Not many people even want to know that they're addicted to suffering, but when you look at it very sincerely, you'll see that many of us have no idea how to live life without suffering. We have no idea how to interact, how to be, what to do with our time and energy if we weren't suffering.

One of the most important steps in the process of coming to the end of suffering is seeing that there's something deep inside of us that actually wants to suffer, that actually indulges in suffering. As I've mentioned, there is a piece of us that wants to suffer because it is through suffering that we maintain this wall of separation around us. It is through our suffering that we can continue to hold onto everything we think is true. Wearing the veil of suffering, we don't really have to look at ourselves and say, "I'm the one that's dreaming. I'm the one that's full of illusions. I'm the one that's holding on with everything I have." It's much easier to see that the other person is caught in illusion. That's easy. "So and so over there, they're completely lost in illusion. They don't know the truth." It's a whole other thing to say, "No, no, no! I'm the one who is caught in illusion. I don't know what's real, I don't know what's true, and part of me actually wants to suffer because then I can remain separate and distinct."

Certainly, on a conscious level, no one wants to suffer, yet we continue to hold onto our ideas, thoughts, and beliefs as if our lives depended upon them. In a certain way, our lives *do* depend on them—not our true lives, but the lives of our egos, the lives of who we think we are. The way we want to see ourselves depends on them. That part of ourself that wants to see itself as separate doesn't really want to merge back with the source, but would rather pay the price and stand up as a separate being, no matter what the cost, and assert its views upon the world.

SUFFERING IS ENTIRELY OPTIONAL

What I am talking about here isn't the kind of self-examination that we're used to. People in the spiritual world are often busy meditating, chanting the name of God, and doing various spiritual practices and prayers as a means of trying to bring happiness to themselves or to garner God's grace. Spiritual people often listen to the teachings of the great awakened ones and try to apply them, but they often miss the key element, and that is: We're addicted to being ourselves. We're addicted to our own self-centeredness. We're addicted to our suffering. We're addicted to our beliefs and our worldview. We really think that the universe would collapse if we relinquished our part in it. In this way, we actually want to continue suffering.

Most addicts come up with a whole variety of reasons why they're addicted, and some of those reasons may be very valid and have some truth to them. But ultimately, at the end of the day, when we're addicted to something, anything, it's because we choose to be. We might blame it on something else, on somebody else, on certain circumstances in our lives—and of course painful moments in our lives might have something to do with our suffering and with the things to which we're addicted. But when it comes to here and now in this moment, the truth is we're not in the past anymore. The truth is that whatever happened, happened. It's past tense, and there's something in us that tends to want to hold onto it, to grasp onto it, mostly because we're terrified to let go of the very things that make us suffer, because if we let go of the past, we wouldn't know who we are anymore. We wouldn't be able to clothe ourselves in the past. We wouldn't be able to feel sorry for ourselves. We would stand in this moment, and this moment only, and we would face ourselves without judgment, shame, or guilt.

I got involved in spirituality at a young age. I was about twenty years old when, for some reason, I just had to know what was true, what was real. I can't tell you all of the reasons that I had to know. I don't even understand them. I literally woke up one morning, and I simply had to know what was ultimately real and true. I knew my life had completely changed, and the orientation that I'd thought my life was based upon was no longer relevant. Something completely new had woken up in my life, and I knew it was going to be about something entirely different than what I had planned on. It was then that I started upon what's called "the spiritual search" and like most other spiritual seekers, I eventually found myself a teacher, and I started meditating.

My teacher was a Zen Buddhist, and in the Zen Buddhist tradition what you do more than anything else is sit around on cushions, stare at the walls, and meditate for hours a day, and so that's what I did. I sat on that cushion, and I tried to meditate, and tried to meditate, and tried to meditate, and tried to meditate. No matter how hard I tried, I was never really, consistently good at it. I never really figured out how to stop my mind. What I often did on the cushion was suffer, not necessarily because of the past, but because I seemed to be completely powerless to break through the view of life that I held onto so tightly.

Somehow, intuitively, I sensed that I wasn't viewing life the way it really was. I had an intuition that there was something else, that there was a different vision, that there was a greater reality than I was currently seeing. I tried everything I knew to break through into that: I meditated and meditated and I wrote in my notebook. I read books. I talked with a multitude of people. And I thought about it in my head, and then I meditated some more, and on and on and on and on it went.

Having grown up an athlete, I knew how to push and strive and struggle for success. The notion of working hard for long periods of time was very familiar to me, so even when it continued to hurt, I could still sit and meditate more. I kept pushing and pushing, as many people do, and after about four years I hit a wall. I realized that I simply couldn't do what I was trying to do. I realized that I didn't really know anything. It took me four years to get to the place where I could say to myself, "I have no idea what I'm doing. I have no idea what's real and what's not real. I have theories; I've written stacks of notebooks on what I think is and isn't real, what I think God is and isn't, but really, at the end of the day, after four years of intense spiritual struggle, I don't know any more than I did at the beginning."

That was a crushing defeat. I didn't know what to do, because I finally knew that I really didn't know the first thing about breaking through into a larger view. I didn't know the first thing about how to stop struggling. I didn't know how to not suffer. I hit a brick wall.

The day I hit the brick wall, I was in my little backyard hut that I had built for my meditation practice, and I sat down on my cushion like I did every other morning. I lit my incense, and I sat down and faced the wall. And just as I began to try to meditate, to try to calm my mind, all of a sudden—from my guts, not from my head, but from deep, deep down within me—something yelled out inside me: "I can't do this anymore! I can't do it! I don't know how to break through! I don't know how to stop struggling. I don't know how to stop striving. I can't do this!" That was the moment. That was the moment when everything began to change. I didn't know it at the time, but everything I'd ever done in my life up until that moment had prepared me to realize that I was powerless, because I was trapped in a certain view of things. Everything I did to try not to suffer, not to struggle, was actually coming from my own viewpoint.

And there was nothing I could do. Finally, I faced the last thing that I ever wanted to face—I think the last thing anybody ever wants to face—and that is absolute, utter, bone-crushing defeat. This is something quite different than feeling despair or despondence. When we feel despair and despondence, we haven't been completely defeated yet, which means we haven't entirely stopped. Something in us is still struggling against what is.

But in that moment where I realized there was literally nothing I could do, everything changed. All of a sudden, my view of everything shifted. Almost like flipping over a card or a coin, everything that I ever thought or felt, everything that I could remember, everything in that moment literally disappeared. I was finally alone. And in this aloneness, I had no idea what I was, or where I was, or what was happening. All I knew was that I had hit the end of some imaginary road. I'd come to some brick wall and found myself suddenly on the other side of it, where the brick wall actually disappeared. And then this great revelation occurred where I realized that I was both nothing and everything, simultaneously.

As soon as that realization came, I started to laugh. I thought, "My God! I've been searching for this for years, meditating for thousands of hours, writing dozens of notebooks—all this searching and all this struggle." It may sound like a short period of time—four years is a relatively short period of time—but when you're in your twenties, four years seems like forever. So in that moment I laughed, because I realized that what I was searching for was always right here, that the enlightenment for which I was seeking was literally the space that I existed in. All along I hadn't ever been far from the end of suffering. It had been an open door from the very beginning, from the first breath that I ever took.

My suffering, as with all suffering, was entirely optional, but I had never known that. What it took to get me to that point was to realize that I couldn't do it, that I couldn't figure it out. That's what it means to stop, or more accurately, that's what it means to *be* stopped, to be completely and utterly stopped. It was a spiritual form of bottoming out, just like what a drug addict might experience. Suddenly I realized that what I was addicted to was me—me, the one who was struggling; me, the one who was striving for enlightenment; me, the one who was confused. I was a junkie for me. Even as I was trying to get beyond myself, to break through to a different view, I couldn't because I was actually addicted to me. And there wasn't a secret about how to get un-addicted. I had to get to the point where I bottomed out, where I stopped, where I realized that I didn't know anything.

I had heard these teachings before, of course. I had heard the teaching of "Don't know. Let go of what you think you know." But I had taken these teachings and conveniently enfolded them into my worldview. I'd thought I understood what the great spiritual teachers were talking about. But at that moment, what I really saw was that I had never understood anything. I had never understood a single thing, and that was quite shocking.

WAKING UP TO REALITY IS NOT A PROCESS

To come to the end of suffering, to experience the beginning of the end, you must go through a type of death. Many spiritual traditions have taught this: you must "die" before you physically die so that you can truly live. If you've ever been with somebody who's close to physical death and who has also completely let go, you know what a state of freedom this can be. It's such an amazing, paradoxical moment, because there the person is, knowing they're going to die, and yet they knew it all along. They knew it their whole life. They knew they were going to die, but they didn't *really* know it until they got some terminal disease, for example, or until the doctor said, "You've got six months to live." For others, the knowledge of death is a certainty: "I'm not going to make it out of here alive." With most people, however, whether they've embraced the idea of death all along or not, there's a turn at the very seat of their consciousness when death looms. What seemed the most horrible thing that could ever happen—physical death—is seen in such a lightness. For some people who are confronted with the immovable barrier of death, death actually becomes their avenue to spiritual awakening and the end of suffering.

My aunt—who was one of my students for many years until she passed away several years ago—worked in hospice care. Once, she was caring for a woman who had terminal cancer and was very close to death. This woman was nearly comatose, unable to communicate any longer. Most of the time she wasn't conscious. One day, the doctors said she only had a few days to live, and the next day quite suddenly, when her kids woke up in the morning, there she was—the same woman who was on her deathbed, who couldn't even speak the day before—out in the living room, running the vacuum cleaner. The kids said, "Mom! What are you doing? How did you get out of bed?"

She said, quite coherently, "I'm vacuuming."

They said, "How could you be vacuuming? You were supposed to be dead by now!"

And she said, "I couldn't die yet, because I don't know who it is that's going to die!"

This story demonstrates the power of something deep within all of us, a deep evolution within our consciousness that is always moving toward completion, toward the realization of what we are, which is itself the only freedom there is. There is relative freedom, there is the relative ending of suffering, and then there is absolute freedom, there is the absolute ending of suffering. These are two very different things. We can always learn different ways and means to modulate or adapt ourselves so we suffer less, so that we make our prison cell of the mind more comfortable. But to make your prison comfortable and to break out of your prison are two different things. That's what happened in this woman: Something deep within her woke up; some deep desire was so alive in her that she wasn't able to die. She first had to really know who she was.

During this time, my aunt said to the woman, "I know just who you should talk to." I'd been teaching for only a couple of years at that point, and I was still working in a machine shop with my father. My aunt called, and she told me the story of this woman. I said, "Well, I have to talk to her. Bring her right over." So my aunt put this woman in her car and drove her over to the shop where I worked. I pulled up two chairs right in the middle of the machine shop in the middle of the day, and we spoke for a while.

She said, "I need to talk to you."

I said, "Okay. What do you need to talk to me about?"

She said, "I'm about to die. I don't know when it's going to be, but I feel it's going to be any day. But I can't die yet, because I don't yet know who I am. I've lived for a long time, and yet I still don't know who I am."

I said, "Well, you've come to the right person." I said, "We'd better get at it, then. You don't have much time, do you?"

She said, "Okay."

I asked her, "Can you drop your entire past, all at once? Can you let yourself see, all at once, that everything that was, everything you ever imagined, is no longer present now? Can you actually enter into this moment fully?"

And she gave a very honest response. She said, "I don't know."

I said, "Well, you'd better hurry up," and that was the conversation. I'm not usually quite that direct with people. I don't usually put them on the spot, immediately, like that, but we both knew that she was going to die and didn't have much time, so there really wasn't time for a process. That was a great benefit to her, because ultimately, waking up to reality and coming to the end of suffering isn't actually a process. This is a very difficult thing for people to realize and truly embody. It's about waking up. There isn't a process of you being asleep at night and then waking up in the morning. You're either asleep or you're awake. And so it is with spiritual awakening. We're either asleep within the dream world of our minds, or we're awake within the true world of reality.

I saw the woman several times over the next week and a half, and at one point I heard that she was feeling ill again, so I went to see her. Sure enough, she was lying in bed again with very little energy, but she had an absolute, fiery, blissful glow in her eye. I didn't even need to ask her. I just said, "You found out, didn't you?"

And she said, "Yes, I did," and she just smiled.

Her husband came in, and he said, "You know, for the last week or so, she's been comforting all of our family and the neighbors! The neighbors have been coming over here, ready to say 'goodbye' to her, but she's been comforting them. She's been telling them that everything will be okay." He said, "It's quite different now. Before, we were trying to comfort her, and now she's trying to comfort us. Isn't that odd? What's happened to her?"

A week and a half before, this was someone who was on her deathbed, and in just a few short days, she had come to a complete stop. Why? Because she didn't have any time. She didn't have time for a process. She didn't have time to figure anything out. She didn't have time to get ready. The time to wake up was now, and the time to let go of her whole life of difficulty was now, and she did. And so, essentially, what this wonderful woman did was what took me almost five years to do. She was able to finally let go.

The truth of the matter is that awakening itself is not a process. There is a process in terms of how we come to express the awakening, but really waking up and coming to the end of our personal suffering is not something that takes time. This fact is very difficult for people to understand. They say, "But Adya, it does take time. It really does take time." What I've found, after meeting with thousands of people around the world, is that those who are still suffering say that it takes time; those that are awake, however, are clear that it doesn't.

So there is somewhat of a conflict here, because our egos, our minds, the little self that we want to protect—these only exist in time. In fact, they depend on time. Our idea of ourselves, of who and what we are, can only continue in time. We often say to ourselves: "Maybe things will be better tomorrow." It's like the addict saying, "Maybe I'll stop drinking tomorrow. Maybe I'll stop taking that drug tomorrow," but what happens tomorrow doesn't come. Days and weeks and months and years go by, but tomorrow is only a repeat of today. Yet when someone gets to that point where there is no tomorrow, where to continue to be an addict is no longer possible, no longer an option, then there's a stopping. It is then that we step outside of time.

TIME IS THE BIGGEST BARRIER TO AWAKENING

Take a moment and imagine that there is no time. Take a moment to just let go of tomorrow. What if letting go of suffering wasn't possible tomorrow—that today, even right now, was all you had, and you had nothing else but today? All of a sudden, you would look at your whole existence through completely different eyes. See if you can feel what it is to exist only now. See what it's like to completely take tomorrow, and yesterday, out of the picture.

Some people fear that to do this would lead to feeling desperation or despondency in life. They kick and scream against the idea: "I couldn't! That would be awful!" But if you feel desperate, despondent, or depressed by this notion, it's because you still haven't removed tomorrow, because that despondency is only an idea that tomorrow will be the same as today. So is it possible for you to remove all notions of tomorrow, just for a moment? Is it really possible to stop and admit that you don't even know how to stop? Nobody knows how to stop. Nobody ever has known how to stop. Tell yourself the truth: You don't know how. Nobody knows how to stop. Nobody knows how to not suffer. Nobody knows how to awaken.

These are all self-evident truths. Everyone knows these truths if they look at them, but who wants to know them? Who wants to know that they don't know how to not suffer? Who wants to know that they don't know how to wake up? But if you let it in, if you really let it in—just like an addict letting in the knowledge that they don't know how to stop—what happens? See if you can taste true stopping, even for a moment. When you stop, do you suffer? Or in the moment of stopping, does suffering disappear?

Your mind may say, "Well, it stopped for this moment, but what about tomorrow?" That means you haven't completely stopped, because in total stopping there is a death. Something dies before you die. What you are can't die, but the idea of yourself is destined to die. There is absolutely nothing that will take the place of really stopping and dying before you die. This is not a physical death I'm talking about. This is a death of who you think you are, of your past and your future. All of that exists only in imagination. Right now, there is always and only freedom and peace. The question is: Is that what you really want?

9

True Autonomy

WHEN I BEGAN my spiritual search at nineteen or twenty years old, I had the idea that when I finally found out what reality was, when I found the enlightenment I was looking for, then that would be it. I imagined that enlightenment was the goal and the end-all. Most of what I'd read in spiritual literature and heard in spiritual teachings reinforced this idea that once you get to enlightenment, it's basically over. You've gone as far as the spiritual life can take you. What I discovered, however, was something quite different.

Once I began to awaken, and once I started to feel a sense of what some of the spiritual teachings might call "enlightenment," my experience was one in which I felt very free and very open. Life was no longer this intimidating event that felt separate from my own being. For a while, that felt totally complete. Like I said, my idea about spirituality was that I would come to this point of enlightenment or freedom, and that would be the goal. I experienced that freedom for quite a while. After a couple of years, however,

I started to feel that there was something else moving, and it carried a feeling of "something's not complete"—even though everything in my experience felt whole and undivided. So to have this feeling that something was not quite done or complete was very odd. Usually, when we have that feeling, our mind interprets it as if there's something more that I have to find, there's something I have to seek, something that's not totally understood. But this feeling of very subtle incompleteness wasn't like that at all. It was more like an intuition that there was more to come—not necessarily more freedom or more enlightenment or more anything in particular, but there was another layer of unfolding that I didn't yet understand.

And then, bit by bit, it began to reveal itself. I began to realize that our spiritual unfolding doesn't really have a goal called "awakening" or "enlightenment." There's not an end point. To spiritually awaken or become enlightened is actually something that allows *another* movement to happen—and another and another and another. Spiritual awakening is the ground from which a whole new movement of spirit starts to occur, and that new movement that comes out of our own sense of freedom is what I call "awakening into our true autonomy."

I realize this might sound odd in the context of teaching on awakening, because we usually think of autonomy as some form of separation. This isn't what I realized. What I realized was that our true autonomy arises from a knowing of unity, of oneness. Even with the realization that everything really is one—even with that—there's still this human element, there's still this being that's been born in time and space. I realized that the ultimate destination of this person born in time and space is not simply to realize this enlightenment, but it is for the purpose of something quite different. In fact, enlightenment makes another movement of consciousness possible. This other movement of consciousness is not really a waking up *from* our humanity, waking up *from* time and space, waking up *from* an individual identity. It is almost the opposite, where spirit comes into form and discovers this true autonomy.

THE UNIQUE FLOWERING OF AN INDIVIDUAL LIFE

To illustrate what I mean by true autonomy, I will use the examples of two of the true spiritual greats in our history: Jesus and the Buddha. We usually think of both Jesus and the Buddha as ones who knew their innate oneness with being. With Jesus, it would be his oneness with God; in Buddha, it would be his enlightenment or his oneness with everything. But this isn't the great realization of these awake beings. There's another reason why we put them on our altars and why so many people worship them and follow their teachings. What I want to suggest here is that it's not just that they realized their oneness with God or their oneness with existence, but both of them, in their own unique way, discovered their own true autonomy.

Jesus is a great example of this. He was someone who really did "stand in his own two shoes," as my teacher would say, which means he occupied his own life. He embodied his humanness in such a way that it didn't cause him to be separate; rather, it allowed spirit to occupy his human life in a very awake way. There's a certain autonomy that comes with that: it's almost as if it allows life to flower in a totally unique way, in a way that's never been. So someone like Jesus was not the outcome of a whole line of others before him. He wasn't the natural extension of what had come before. Rather, he embodied a radical breaking away from the past. He brought in a whole new revelation—something extraordinarily unique and very dynamic.

In conventional terms, Jesus brought forward his "mission in life." Our egos usually think of missions as something along the lines of "what we're meant to do," or "what we're supposed to do," which is, in large part, a mentally created idea. The discovery of one's true autonomy isn't something that the ego or the mind does. It's actually a flowering of existence in a very creative and new way. It was Jesus's willingness to live out that unique expression of oneness, to live that unique expression of God, in form, that was so transformative.

Since the time he lived, we've made Jesus into a projection of what we would hope an awake or God-realized being would be. And in doing so, we've sanitized him from what he seems to actually have been. When we read about the life of Jesus—what he did, how he acted, how he moved through the world of time and space—we see someone who doesn't conform to our conventional ideas of what it means to be awake. Yet, Jesus was an extremely dynamic personality, somebody with great vigor and a real fearlessness to allow spirit to manifest as it wished, which is really what true autonomy is. There's a way in which life is trying to express itself through each of us, but it has a hard time doing it in a clear way when we're identified with the egoic state of consciousness. That energy gets distorted, and it gets boxed into very familiar patterns that are old and repetitive. Jesus woke up to an innate freedom, and it was that freedom that then allowed life or spirit to flower and express itself in a totally new way. It's this that connects with people in an intuitive way, in an unconscious way. And this is the reason why people have put Jesus on altars and devoted themselves to him through the ages.

The same thing happened with the Buddha. The Buddha had his great enlightenment under the *bodhi* tree—that's what the story says—and yet the Buddha didn't just rest there in some great state of composure and bliss for the rest of his life. He actually lived out a very dynamic life in which he was teaching and bringing forward something very fresh, something that people had never heard before. It was a new manifestation of spirit into time and space. It was that willingness to be who he was—not only in his essence, but also in his human expression—that really compels us and speaks to us throughout all the centuries.

It is important to see that neither one of these figures moved through life in the way that we tend to imagine. I've seen movies, spiritual epics, about the life of Jesus and they often project Jesus to be a very saintly figure, walking on water, performing miracles. They portray someone who is almost otherworldly. And yet, when we read the story of who Jesus actually was, it paints a very different picture. Jesus was someone who moved in life in a way that was quite contrary to the spiritual norms of his time. He found his students among fishermen and tradesmen; he didn't pick them from nobility. He walked among people who were not necessarily spiritual or pious souls, but rather very ordinary working-class people whom he picked as his core disciples.

When we look closely at the way he lived his life, we see him eating and socializing among the common people, spending time with prostitutes, with people who'd broken the law, and with people who had cheated on their husbands and wives. He had parties, where people would come together and celebrate; they'd drink wine and at times he would get extraordinarily angry. The most well-known example of Jesus's anger is when he kicked over the money changers' tables right outside the temple. I've often thought: I wonder what would happen in a church today if somebody were making money in a way that someone like Jesus wouldn't approve of. What if that someone walked into the church and literally kicked over the tables? Is that somebody that we would revere? Is that someone that we would think was holy and inspired by God? And yet the story tells us that Jesus did do something very similar to that. What we see is Jesus as a human being, someone who could even get angry.

In almost every story of the religious greats, the spiritual geniuses, most of the humanness is actually whitewashed out of the story. In the way the Buddha's life is traditionally portrayed, we don't really find the Buddha having any truly difficult moments, such as being very emotional, or having much despair. A very common motif throughout all the religions is to have the holy figures be almost otherworldly. But the powerful thing about the Jesus story is that he had some very human and very intense emotions. There was a time when he was in the Garden of Gethsemane, and he had a foretelling of his destiny to be crucified. When he saw that, he literally begged God to see if he could get out of it, if somehow his destiny could be changed. This isn't something you would expect out of your holy man. Jesus knew he had a destiny. He knew he had to go through certain things, and he knew, because spirit had manifested as a human being, that he was both human *and* divine.

THE WILLINGNESS TO OCCUPY THIS LIFE

To be human is also to open ourselves up to very human experiences. The strength and the character of someone like Jesus is revered not because he never felt anguish or frustration. He is revered because even though he did feel challenged at times, and at times felt great despair, he still followed through with his destiny. He was still a very autonomous person. He didn't try to escape from his life, from his existence. He didn't try to run inside to some meditative state that would ensure him that he'd never have to feel the ups and downs of human life and human affairs. And through his human experience, he was able to manifest something quite extraordinary, a very extraordinary life, a teaching that was quite unique and dynamic.

To be born as a human, to take this particular form, is to be challenged. Even for the awakened ones, life is not always smooth. As I like to remind people, even when enlightenment comes, even when you realize the innate and natural freedom of being, it doesn't get you a pass on life. It doesn't mean you're never going to go through anything difficult. Quite the opposite. The more awake we become, often the more capable we are of having life hand us bigger and bigger situations as our capacity to accept and embody our spiritual essence grows. So life can and does respond to that growth, and in many ways it tends to demand more and more from us.

This isn't what a lot of people have in mind when they think of spiritual freedom. Generally, it seems most people have the idea that I used to have about spiritual freedom, which is that freedom is defined by what we're free *from*. In other words, we can be so transcendent that we're literally free from life. But at some point in time, we come to see that this is a relatively immature idea of what freedom is. Only an immature idea of freedom is defined by what we're free from. Something more mature, something that develops and grows within us as we become more spiritually mature is not a freedom *from,* but a freedom *to.* We can look at it this way: Are we free enough and open enough *to* meet life? A big enough freedom to live life, to really "stand in our own two shoes," to actually occupy the ground on which we stand? Even though we're not separate, even though the whole universe is contained within us, there's still a human component, an individual person with the capacity to allow spirit to flow out into the world. We can either open to this or shy away from it.

All along the way on our spiritual journey, often without even knowing it, we're discovering what our true autonomy is. When people come to see me, I tell them that it's essential that they begin to step into their autonomy, not at the end of a spiritual process, not at the end of some event called "spiritual awakening" or "enlightenment," but right at the very beginning.

One of the things that we all do when we get exposed to spiritual teachings, especially teachings that we don't particularly understand, is that we abdicate our own authority. I see it all the time when I speak with people. A lot of people who come to hear me are trying to abdicate their authority. They're trying to give it over to me, and I'm often saying to them, "No. You can't do that." You can't do that, even at the very beginning, because to think that we're going to ride on the coattails of some spiritual teacher to enlightenment is a great delusion. It doesn't work that way. To wake up, to find out what enlightenment is, to touch upon the ending of our suffering, requires us to have the willingness to occupy this life, to occupy our incarnation, without grasping at it or identifying with it. We must find a way to stand up tall, but without saying "It's me!" or "Mine!" exclusively. Taking our seat in our own true autonomy is not just something that happens at the end of the spiritual search. It's necessary right from the beginning.

One way to evaluate whether a spiritual teaching is a skillful one or not is by seeing if it helps you listen to your own inner wisdom. It will tell you if you're getting a little off balance, a little too far left, or a little too far right off the path. A true spiritual teaching will never take anyone's autonomy; it won't require us to give away our good sense. Yes, don't grasp your judging ideas, don't stick with your limited opinions, but also don't abdicate your own authority because there is something within everyone, even at the start of their search for freedom, that has a stand in truth, an intuitive sense of what's real or not real. It may be hard to find initially, but a good spiritual teaching helps you to hone in on your own truth—to become quiet and to listen deeply and openly enough so that you can literally begin to feel the way life is informing you. That's your inner wisdom. That's your inner teacher, and it's the beginning of standing in your true autonomy.

OUR PREFERENCES PLAY NO PART IN THE SPIRITUAL LIFE

In this process of waking up and coming into our true autonomy, it's very easy to get out of balance. Sometimes we'll grasp too much of our autonomy before we're ready to handle it. Once my teacher sent me to another teacher to do my first Zen retreat because I'd said that I wanted to do a traditional retreat. So I packed my bags and I drove up to a Zen temple in Sonoma, California. It was at the top of a mountain, and I was so excited to be there! I had anticipated being there for a couple of years, and here I was at this very traditional Zen temple, and I was just about to begin my first Zen *sesshin* (or "retreat"). I knew that Zen retreats were known to be quite austere and rigorous, and the schedule required us to meditate at least nine times a day, every day, and all through the night on the last day. I looked at this sesshin with almost mythic eyes, through all the stories I'd heard about what happens on these retreats.

I'll never forget the first private meeting with the teacher. He asked me how I meditated, and so I told him. I told him how I was just basically sitting in silence and more or less following my own inner guidance as to what seemed to be the right thing to do. When I explained this, he looked at me very sternly, and he said, "You didn't come here to do what you want to do. You came here so that I could help guide you. Which is it that you want?"

I remember feeling quite taken aback. At my very first meeting with the teacher, he was drawing this line between us, and he was basically saying, "Your ego has no part here." I was shocked, because I'd listened to him give talks, and he was quite sweet and kind and warm. Now here he was laying a demand upon me at our very first meeting. I thought about it for a few seconds, and I realized, "You know, he's right. I didn't come all this way just to do everything the way I think it should be done. I could have done that at home. I could have stayed right where I was and done it the way I wanted to do it." So I said, "I think I'll listen here. I think I'll try to do what you suggest."

The teacher told me about a meditation technique that sounded quite boring, not very interesting at all. What he wanted me to do with each out-breath, was to count "one," and then with the next out-breath "two," and with the next out-breath "three," until I got to "ten," and then I'd start back at "one" again. He had a very specific way he wanted me to sit, with my back upright, my shoulders tucked back, my chin tucked in, and my hands in what's called a *mudra,* a specific meditative position for the hands and fingers. It all seemed quite technical, but I had decided I came here to see what this man had to teach me, so I did as he suggested.

After three or four days, I had another meeting with him, and once again he asked how my meditation was going. He had me sit on a cushion, because he wanted to see the posture of my body. He wanted to see how I was holding my hands in the mudra. He looked at me, and he made some corrections. And then we talked a little bit, and he asked about my experience with counting the breath. I said, "Well, it's really quite boring, and what I find is I keep getting lost, even before I get to 'ten.'"

He said, "That's quite natural. Don't worry about it. When you get lost, just start at 'one' again; don't worry about it. Just let it go," and so I said I would.

I went home from that retreat a couple of days later, after it ended, and I decided that I was going to keep doing the meditation that he had taught me. After a few months, I wrote him a letter. I said, "I've been doing this meditation that you've asked me to do, and I'll be happy to continue doing it if you think I should, but I'm getting this intuition that maybe I could let go of the counting of my breaths. I don't know if it's the right thing to do or not, but it's my intuition that maybe it's good for me to just be silent instead of counting my breaths." At the end of the letter,

I wrote, "But if you think that's not a correct thing to do, then let me know," and I sent it off.

I got a letter back about a week later. The teacher just made a quick comment on the side of my letter, and he said, "That sounds good to me. That's okay. Do it that way." It was my first understanding of what it was to be in a true relationship to a spiritual teacher. What he did on our first meeting was more important than the fact that he told me about a certain meditation technique. There was actually something much more significant that was happening at the time. What he was telling me, in essence, without really telling me directly, was that my ego, my preferences, played no part in the spiritual life, that he was not going to follow around my ego's wants and desires, that our relationship was not going to be based in this. He drew a line in the sand. But as I let go of my ego a bit and started to listen to what he had to say, I then received an intuition and guidance from my inner teacher. It was then that he started to give back the authority that he'd taken away on our first meeting. It was very skillful and very wise. A true teacher will always be trying to give your authority back to you as fast as you can receive it—and without becoming egoically self-centered again.

When people first come to see me, I always tell them that they're going to have to begin to find this true autonomy and true authority within themselves. I'll be happy to help them find it, because it is easy to lose the way. But it's important to know in spirituality that you have to let go of all ideas of totally abdicating your authority, of abdicating responsibility for yourself and giving it to a spiritual teacher—or anybody else, for that matter. What's really important is that we have the capacity to open and to listen, that we have the ability to be available, to hear things that we're not used to hearing, to see things in new ways. A spiritual teaching should actually challenge us, challenge our views, challenge the way we think. If it simply conforms to our views and the way we think, it's really not any good to us, because it will just reinforce our illusions of separation and superiority.

ALLOWING TRUE AUTONOMY TO FLOWER

So how do we find our true autonomy? It is important to remember that autonomy isn't the same as separation. In fact, it has nothing to do with separation. True autonomy is not about "me" as an ego; it's about life itself. It's spirit embodying form, inhabiting a human life, and standing up in that form. The paradox is that first we often awaken *from* form. We come to realize that we can't be defined by our bodies, minds, egos, and personalities. That's why the term "waking up" is so instructive: we're literally waking up *from* identity, from who we think we are. We're also waking up from all the ideas that culture has placed within us and all the emotions to which we've become addicted.

Many things are within us from which to awaken, but that's not the completion of the spiritual journey. We actually wake up, which is almost like an up-and-out process. Literally, the energy within us goes up and out. Eventually, what will happen is that same energy, that same consciousness, will then come down and in. It will begin to move in a different way. It will come back down and back into form, back into our humanness. Spirit comes back, as it were, to itself—back into body, back into mind, and back into our human life. In so doing, it begins to realize and awaken to its true autonomy, a sense of being that is quite independent, while not being separate.

It's important that we don't make up ideas about all this, that we don't create a whole theory or theology about how spirit should manifest, about how it should discover its own true autonomy. Because as soon as we do that, then we're back in the mind, and we've lost our freedom and illumined creativity. Of course, we can still access our minds. In this way, the mind is a beautiful tool. But if we're used by it, we'll quickly find ourselves back in the spinning web of egoic consciousness. We can't have an idea of what life should look like, about how spirit should be manifesting as our very life, because all of those ideas would just be products of the past—something we learned, imagined, or desired. Once again, we find ourselves back in the unknown—not in the idea of the unknown, but in the lived reality of it. It's the mind humbled, on its knees, with bare feet and free of the known.

FINDING THE TRUTH WITHIN YOURSELF

The first time I went to see my teacher, it was a very odd experience. I had found her name in the back of a book, and I couldn't believe that there was a Zen teacher fifteen minutes from where I was living. What great good fortune to have a Zen master almost around the corner! And I remember the enormous anticipation I felt the day that I went to meet her. It was a Sunday morning, because she always met with students on Sunday mornings, and I was driving up through the foothills of Los Gatos. I was following the directions she had given me, but it seemed very strange, like I had made some sort of wrong turn. I can't really tell you why, but I was going down dirt roads and obscure paved roads, and for some reason—maybe I was nervous, who knows?—I kept getting lost.

Eventually, I found the way, by accident it seemed. The first surprise was that this Zen teacher was teaching out of her home! I had expected a temple, monks in traditional robes, and all the rest, and yet here was an ordinary home in the foothills of Los Gatos. I parked the car on the side of the road, and I walked up the driveway. It was a very strange driveway; I couldn't figure out where the front door of the home was. Most homes have an obvious entry, an obvious front door, but her front door was not facing the road. It was actually facing inward, toward the driveway. It took me a while to find it because there were a number of doors. I didn't even know it was the front door until I grabbed the handle, and then I noticed there was a sign draped over the handle, and it said, "Zazen," with an arrow pointing toward a gate. So I went through the gate, through the back yard, up some steps, onto a deck, and then I saw the sliding glass doors in her back yard.

There were only two people there: a woman and a middle-aged man. I walked up to the door, knocked, and she opened it. She looked at me and said, "Welcome." She pointed to my shoes, and then she told me where to put my shoes. I kicked off my shoes to the side of the door, and she said, "Oh, no, no! Please put your shoes nice and straight," so I straightened them up, and I walked in the door. What I didn't know at the time was that I was receiving my first teaching. By pointing out my shoes and that I'd just kicked them off, and her request to straighten them up, she was actually beginning to teach me about my life, to take care of my life, to be aware, to be conscious of what I was doing. Without saying it, what she was really saying was, "Be aware of your shoes. Stay conscious. Stay awake. Don't go to sleep to anything."

Next I walked into the kitchen, and she pointed toward the living room. In the living room, a lot of the furniture was moved out, and there were cushions set up for meditation. The space was very, very beautiful, and there was a small statue of a Buddha figure at the far end of the room. At home I'd sit on this furry blanket that had a big picture of a lion on the front. I had come with that blanket all folded up, and when I turned the corner into the living room and saw all of the beautiful cushions and a number of people settling into the room, I looked down at my blanket and felt suddenly like a child carrying his blankie to this great meditation center. I was so embarrassed that I walked over to a wall and put the blanket behind me, and I tried to drop it at my feet without anybody noticing. This was another teaching: the teaching of humility. Of course, at the time I didn't know that any of these were teachings; only in retrospect did I become aware of them.

I took my seat, the bell was rung, and we began meditation. I didn't know at the time, but that was the beginning of a thirteen-year student-teacher relationship with my teacher. What she showed me during those thirteen years was how, at each step, to find my true autonomy. Whenever I'd ask her a question, she'd point me inside, and she'd say, "What do you think?"

I'd come to her, confused, and say, "I'm not sure if I'm meditating very well. Can you help me?"

She'd say, "Well, what are you doing?" I'd say I'm doing this, or doing that, and she'd say, "Well, what do *you* think you should do?" and I'd say this or that, and sometimes she'd make a little suggestion. She'd say, "Oh, maybe a little bit more like this. Maybe a little bit more like that." It was always just a suggestion.

She had a different way of teaching than the Zen teacher at the retreat center I was to go to a couple of years later, but in essence, she was easing me into my own autonomy, my own authority. For many years, I found it frustrating that I never got a real straight answer from her, or at least I didn't think I did. When I would meet with her in private and ask her certain questions about my spiritual life, she would always help direct me back into myself, when what I wanted was a nice, clear, concise spiritual answer that I could hold in my mind with certainty. She never even once gave this to me—not in thirteen years of being together. It took me a long time to realize that this was a great gift she was giving me. She was insisting that I find the truth inside myself. She refused to give me a teaching that my mind would hold onto and grasp. She just pointed me deeper inside, and through that, I found that I developed a capacity to listen inside, and to follow, and to find out what was true and not true, and wise and not wise.

LISTENING IS THE FIRST STEP

Again, I didn't understand what my teacher was doing until many years later—that she was trying to help me discover my own innate autonomy right from the beginning. Because she refused to take all the authority away from me, she pushed me deeper and deeper into the truth of myself, so I could find my own way. This is one of the sobering realities of waking up, of shifting out of the egoic state of consciousness and into our true nature: No one can tell you exactly how to do it. It's not like following a recipe where if you just listen to the teacher and do exactly what you're told and nothing else, and never think for yourself, that you'll become enlightened. It doesn't work that way. We have to discover something in ourselves, intuitively, something that our minds can't quite grasp. From the very beginning, we have to be feeling our way in the dark for our true inner wisdom.

My teacher used to say, "It's like looking for a pillow that you lost in the middle of the night. You just reach behind your head, your hand falls right on it, and you just find it." I understood this because I've lost my pillow in the middle of the night a number of times in my sleep.

Often I wake up, and inevitably, even though I can't see anything because it is dark, my hand reaches out and goes right to the pillow. So, using these common expressions, I was being taught to trust myself, that there is something within each of us that can find its way. What we've really got to do is stop listening to our minds. We instead need to listen to the silence inside, listen in that place where our listening takes us beyond what we think we know.

This is true even when we're in dense states of suffering, when we're very much tied up in a knot, when we're in turmoil, deep sadness, grief, or depression. Strangely, the more we struggle to get out of these states, the deeper we sink into them. The more we try to figure them out, the more we make ourselves confused, when what we really need to do is to begin to listen. Listening is the first step in discovering our autonomy, an autonomy that, if we take this search for our own happiness and freedom all the way, will fully flower one day into something we can't imagine. But at the beginning, you've got to start by taking the little steps, and the first way is to begin to really, deeply listen. Develop an intuition of what you need to attend to, what you need to question, what assumptions you need to take a second look at. This is just the beginning of discovering a certain autonomy. Mistakes will be made, and you will go down wrong roads, but that's how we find out where our true autonomy lies.

It's somewhat like finding balance when you're learning to ride a bicycle. Nobody can teach you how to balance on a bicycle. They can give you suggestions, but essentially, you have to simply push off on your own. Sometimes you lose balance and start to fall, but others can catch you so you won't hurt yourself. To find our true autonomy, our inner balance so to speak, we must really listen—at deeper and deeper and deeper levels. What is it that silence is trying to tell you that you may not be listening to?

Another way to explore our true autonomy is through this inquiry: What do you know that you may not want to know? Because we're all wiser than we pretend to be, and much of the time our wisdom is in those places where we know things that aren't comfortable for us, that aren't convenient for us. If we listened to these places, we know that they'd pull us out of hiding, force us to deal with some situation, or with some emotional state within us. Ultimately, real autonomy is a complete allowing of spirit to inhabit your humanness and a fearless willingness to allow this freedom to happen.

There is a freedom to love, a freedom to engage, a freedom even to be disturbed, and a freedom, ultimately, that allows life to bloom within us, that allows spirit to flow through us in a completely unknown way. This freedom is unknown to such an extent that you really don't know what you're meant to be, because you're too busy being it! If someone were to ask me, "Adya, what is it that you've found that you're meant to be, that you're meant to do, that spirit is really meant to accomplish through you?" the most I could say is, "This moment is it. This moment is it, and in the next moment, that's it. And in the next moment, that's it."

LOVE AS THE FIERCE EMBRACE OF LIFE

Our autonomy is discovered in each and every moment. It requires a fierce embrace of life and of our existence, because the true expression of our spiritual nature is love, and love isn't what we think it is. *Love* is synonymous with this fierce embrace of life. Love is seeing yourself as everything and as everybody, and that seeing is not for your mind. It's not meant for your ego. You can never see all as one with your ego. You can only see it from your essence.

Take someone like Jesus. His life was an expression of love—both in its ups and downs, and in the wonderful miracles and the very challenging moments. All of it was life's expression of love, and human beings have benefited from that story for more than two thousand years. Jesus's life was a gift, and yours is a gift just as much. It doesn't mean you're going to be a great teacher, or that you're going to be well known. It doesn't have anything to do with becoming a celebrity or being remembered in history. That may happen. That may not happen. As long as you care about being remembered or being significant, you haven't totally let go. What if you found out that the way spirit wanted to manifest through you was as a simple, ordinary person, but a person with great love, great compassion, and great wisdom? Maybe nobody would even recognize you. Nobody would acknowledge it in you, but it would simply be who and what you are. What if that were the way life wanted to manifest through you? Would that be okay with you? Would you allow it to happen?

It's only our egos and our minds that think of this whole notion of autonomy in egoic ways. It's obvious that someone like a Jesus or a Buddha didn't care how people viewed them. They didn't care about being remembered. They weren't trying to accomplish any of that. They were dynamic forces of love and spiritual enlightenment in the world of time and space. They had surrendered and let go to the truth within us all, and their lives were dedications, expressions, and embodiments of that realization of love. Remember, Jesus wasn't loved by everybody. His teaching got him killed! He didn't walk around having everybody fall at his feet. Far from it! So any idea of what an awakened life should look like is just an idea, just an imagination, and as long as we're trying to make our lives look like anything other than what they are, then we're lost. We're just spinning in our own imagination.

The true significance of any of our lives is something that's very, very close. It's in each breath you take. It's the manifestation of that stillness within you. It's the unborn birthing itself, moment to moment. There's no "how to," and there's no such thing as what it should look like. I can't teach anybody how to do it. I can only tell you that it's possible. You can feel it. You've felt it your whole life. You've always known there's something inside of you that's sought to be born, fresh and real. You know there's something inside you, far beyond your imagination, that's been trying to break out and be. Everyone feels this inside. But to allow life to express itself in that way, with that much abandon, requires a true surrender into the unknown. We must let go of even the great realizations or awakenings we have. Even the greatest wisdom that comes to you, the greatest "Ah-hah!" was meant for that moment and that moment only.

The invitation is for all of us to stay in beginner's mind, to always stay in touch with the unborn, the undying, and the uncreated, because it's from that potential that something in us awakens that is free from strife and suffering and that has been waiting in every single one of us to express itself. The great sages of our collective history have all told us that what they realized is meant for each one of us, that it's not unique to them. It's not something they own. It's something they realize is inherent within everything and everybody, because really, it's not you or I who wake up. It's life that wakes up. Your life becomes an expression of that which is inexpressible, unexplainable, and indefinable.

10

Beyond the World of Opposites

IN RECENT TIMES, there was a sage in India named Nisargadatta Maharaj. I read a discussion he had with a woman, and she was telling him about how she saw the world, about the suffering and striving, the violence and the anger and the greed, and her own inner world of turmoil. She asked him how he interacted in that world, and he said something very surprising. He said, "That's your world. I don't exist in your world. I don't even know your world. In my world, none of that exists."

It took me aback when I read this. I thought, "What does he mean that he doesn't exist in that world, that his world is something else?" It brought to mind another saying that's very well known, where Jesus says, "I am in the world, but not of it." This is a very similar kind of saying. There's a deep truth that's being revealed through both of these teachings. What is this world that Nisargadatta said he's not in, and that Jesus was referring to when he said, "I'm in it, but not of it?"

Of course they're talking about our world, the one in which most human beings exist when we open our eyes, go about our lives, and have interactions. That's the world that Jesus was saying, "I'm in it, but not of it." The world most humans are in is the world of relativity, of light and dark, of good and bad, of love and hate. This is the world that most of us are born into: the world of opposites. In fact, the manifest world around us is nothing but the inter-action of opposites: of nighttime turning to daytime, daytime turning back to nighttime, of love and hate, of breathing in and breathing out, of good and bad, of should and shouldn't. Everything in the manifest world operates through this flux and flow of opposites. In some ways, these distinctions are necessary. Life itself couldn't exist without opposites, without night and day, without breathing in and breathing out. If you look closer, you'll find that within most human beings, we find the same opposites: the good and the bad, the right and the wrong, what I should and what I shouldn't do, what I imagine should happen and what shouldn't happen. This world of opposites informs the functioning of our minds; it provides a framework in which our minds can operate. So how can these sages say that this is not the world that's true to them, not the world where they essentially are? They may operate in this world; they may seem to exist in it, but really, where their consciousness is, where their real home is, is in another world.

It's vitally important that we understand these two worlds. The conventional world is the world of our imagination—of duality, of right and wrong. This is the world in which we most often interact. When our minds operate in this relative world, our only choice is to relate to life in terms of opposites. The egoic state of consciousness is defined by duality—good and bad, right and wrong, form and formlessness, spirit and matter. This is the state of consciousness that we're in when we're identified with ego. It's the state of consciousness where it's always either "this" *or* "that." It's not "this" *and* "that." Either I'm right or I'm wrong. Either you're right or you're wrong.

There is a whole other state of consciousness, a state of consciousness that isn't of the world of duality. This is the state of consciousness that Jesus referred to as "the kingdom of Heaven." The kingdom of Heaven is really the state of consciousness that's beyond duality, that's not living within the confines of duality. As a person, Jesus clearly existed within the world of duality, but his consciousness was obviously somewhere else. His consciousness was in "the kingdom of Heaven," what the Buddha called *nirvana*. Nirvana refers to complete freedom from the "wheel of suffering" and life lived outside the egoic state of consciousness altogether. The Buddha, being off the wheel of suffering, was no longer living from the perspective of right and wrong, good and bad, light and dark. When we begin to wake up from the egoic state of consciousness, we release the view of life that's confined to relative viewpoints.

Interestingly, there is something about this, to our minds, that sounds dangerous. What could it mean to be beyond right and wrong, beyond good and bad? Wouldn't that just lead to chaos? What would be the principle upon which human beings lived? What would keep us from acting in unkind and hurtful ways? But of course, those kinds of questions come from the limitations of egoic consciousness, which is an expression of relativity. Egoic consciousness can't even imagine another state. All it can do is project its own understanding of another state, but it can never actually attain it. Spiritual awakening isn't for our egos. It's for our deeper, inner nature. It's for the source and substance of what we really are.

TO ABIDE IN NON-ABIDING

Many years ago, I was staying at a Buddhist monastery, and the abbess there—a wonderful, wise woman—made a very interesting observation. She said, "Everybody knows not to get caught in Hell, but very few people know how not to get caught in Heaven."

At the time I heard that, I didn't really understand it. First, I thought, "Well, yeah, our instinct isn't to get caught in Hell, but a lot of people do." Then I thought, "Why wouldn't somebody want to be caught in Heaven? Why wouldn't somebody want to be caught in enlightenment?"

This seemed to be a very strange thing she was saying: "Don't get caught in Heaven." It took me many years before I realized, myself, what she meant by this. Because if we get caught in Heaven, it's just as limiting as getting caught in

Hell. It would almost be like saying, "Breathe out a great sense of 'Aaaaaaaaaaaah!' It feels so good to breathe out, so the goal is to breathe out." But if all we did was breathe out, we'd die pretty soon. We have to breathe in so that we can breathe out. They go together, like a right hand and a left hand, like up and down on a see-saw. When we're in egoic consciousness, we're always trying to move away from what we think is bad, toward what we imagine to be good. But of course, what we imagine to be good is also intimately linked with the appearance of what's bad.

No matter how far or how deep our spiritual realization goes, it's always important to know how not to get caught in Heaven or Hell—actually, to never be caught anywhere. As one old, wise, Zen master said, "to abide in non-abiding." Jesus referred to this state that's beyond the pairs of opposites when he said, "The foxes have their holes in the ground and the birds have their nests in the trees, but the Son of Man has nowhere to rest his head." It was his way of reminding people that where he is, the kingdom of Heaven, isn't really heavenly. It's beyond Heaven and Hell. It's beyond the pairs of opposites. We've turned Jesus's Heaven into the opposite of Hell, but clearly, for Jesus, the kingdom of Heaven wasn't something that's confined or even defined by the pairs of opposites. For him, the kingdom of Heaven was something entirely different. It was a state of consciousness that wasn't caught within the dualistic point of view at all.

The dualistic point of view is very tricky and very subtle. Many of the classical spiritual teachings point us away from the mind and the body—away from identification with all form. The ancient teachings would say, "You are not this. You are not that. You are not your body. You are not your mind. You are not what you think." This has been referred to as "the Negative Way," the way of negation. The Negative Way shows up in different forms of Hinduism, Buddhism, and also in Christianity. There's a way that these teachings point us away from attachment with all form, both gross and subtle, so that we can realize and wake up to our source as spirit, as presence, as that open field of awareness, which is not a "thing" at all. It's more like a great, awake, and alive nothing. But if we were to just try to hold onto that, then we would just be deluding ourselves once again. It may be a higher level of delusion than being caught in the egoic state of consciousness, but it's a state of delusion nonetheless, because it's not complete. It's just the opposite of the egoic state. The formless state of consciousness is just the opposite of that state of consciousness which is identified with form.

Ultimately, the idea isn't to go from identification with form to identification with formlessness. It's not about going from a somebody to a nobody. You can't define the truth as something, or as nothing. You can't ultimately define it as spirit or as matter. You can't define it as ego or other than ego. Our ultimate nature can't be described in dualistic terms at all. To our minds, it will always remain a mystery, because the process of thought that we use to apprehend things can only think in dualistic terms. So our minds can never really know reality directly. Even on the level of our feelings, we feel good or we feel bad. We feel open, or we feel closed. We feel happy, or we feel sad. Even our emotions, at least the majority of them, are expressions of duality.

In many forms of spirituality, you get the impression that there's almost a condemnation of life and the realm of formlessness is really what it's all about. But if we get attached to the formless, to the inner spaciousness of being, to that pure consciousness—even though it's much more free, open and spacious—if we get caught there, we've just settled for another, higher level delusion. So what is this truth that Jesus was speaking about, to be "in this world, but not of it"? What is this truth that he was expressing in the story of the foxes having their holes in the ground, and the birds in the trees, but the Son of Man having nowhere to rest his head? The teaching here is concerned with relativity: high and low, something and nothing, spirit and matter. What Jesus is saying here is that what he is is beyond this—and not just beyond it, but also including it.

The Buddha was asked one day, as he was walking down the road, "What are you? Are you a man?"

The Buddha said, "No. I am not a man."

The Buddha was then asked, "Are you an animal?"

The Buddha said, "No, I'm not an animal."

"Well, then, are you a God?"

"No, I am not a God."

The person asked, in great frustration, "Well, what is it that you are?"

He simply said, "I am awake."

That was the Buddha's way of pointing beyond all definitions, beyond all descriptions. This state of consciousness is the hardest place to describe, because it is literally indescribable. The highest reality is being both "this" and "that" and neither; being both spirit and human; being a field of open, spacious awareness, as well as one particular human incarnation. This is something that takes great subtlety, a deep willingness to go beyond all of our notions, even our notions of good and bad, and right and wrong.

One of the Taoist masters said, "When the Great Way is lost, good and evil are created." "The Great Way" refers to the ultimate truth, the ultimate reality. When you and I become unconscious of the Great Way beyond all duality, then we have to create conventions like good and bad. In the relative world, that's a reasonable thing to do. It's reasonably better to be good than bad—that just makes sense—but in the ultimate state of reality, it's neither good nor bad. It's something that's beyond.

THE VIRGIN BIRTH: BEYOND THE PAIRS OF OPPOSITES

You can find common themes throughout many of the world's religions: Christianity, Buddhism, Islam, Hinduism, as well as those that existed long before modern religious history. One of the more common motifs that appears cross-culturally is that of the virgin birth. We all know the story of Jesus and how he was said to have been born of a virgin. In Buddhism we also have the story of Buddha being born from his mother's side. Both of these stories are simply ways of communicating a deeper truth.

We're usually taught to focus on the historical aspects of these births—what happened and whether somebody was or wasn't a virgin. But this misses the point. If we just look at the historical facts of some religion and try to decide whether they're right or wrong, we miss the significance of the teaching. These stories of virgin birth refer to the birth of that which is born without the coming together of opposites. Our human birth is the birth of opposites. It's the coming together of male and female, and that produces a human being. Our humanness is a manifestation of the opposites, our hearts beating, opening and closing, our lungs breathing in and then out and then in and out. So our physical birth is always a birth of opposites, which is quite beautiful in and of itself. The whole world around us is the manifestation of opposites, no matter what its expression. But this notion of the virgin birth addresses our "second" birth, our birth after we were born. It's the birth, in our consciousness, of a vision that's not based in duality. These stories recognize that what we really are is in fact the source of all opposites, of both male and female, both this and that. It's the birth of a unified vision right into this world of time and space.

Jesus's virgin birth is trying to tell us that this person, Jesus, the Christ, was really a manifestation of what was beyond the pairs of opposites. And that person is also you. Certainly he had a human body and a human mind, just like you. In fact, he referred to himself as "the son of man." Later, others began to refer to him as "the son of God." Jesus knew that he had a human body and mind, and yet his consciousness was not of the world of opposites. The virgin birth points to our own awakening from the ego.

At the moment of awakening, it literally feels like we're being born again, or like something completely new and unexpected has shown up in our consciousness. It literally is a virgin birth—a birth not of duality, but a birth of nonduality, a birth of that which is far beyond all dualities.

We don't have to go a long way to find this virgin birth; we can investigate our experience right here and now. Like everything else in truth, it's already present. If you look into this moment and become quiet and sensitive, you can intuitively feel that there's something about you, right here and right now, that's not definable as male or female, as this or that. There's something about you that's not definable at all. There is already a sense in you of that which cannot be defined by any words. That's the consciousness that's birthing itself into recognition, possibly at this very moment. It may start out as just a glimpse, a taste, a feel, but if you give great attention to it, a recognition dawns that there it is, in your experience right now.

The fact that our true nature is ultimately nondual is precisely why when we're born into this material world we find ourselves attracted to our opposite. It doesn't mean that all men are attracted to women, or all women are attracted to men, but if you really look at the deep intimate or romantic relationships of human beings, you'll see that there's often something in you that is attracted to your opposite, something that you don't feel like you have. That's our spirit's deep desire for union, for coming together, for remembering our unified nature. Always there is that which is neither male nor female, but both and beyond. All you have to do is turn, right in the moment, into the depth of your own experience to see this. Let go of your mind trying to define anything, and you'll see for yourself that what you really are is something beyond all definition.

There's a wonderful quote from a very famous Zen master called Huang Po. What it describes is the unity of spirit, that our truest nature is neither this nor that, but both. It also elegantly describes the natural nobility found in all of reality. To begin to experience the truth of what Huang Po is saying here, you must understand how he is using the word "mind." He uses it in the way that we use the words "consciousness" or "spirit." By "mind," he's not referring to the thinking process, but to the context in which all form, including thought itself, appears. He said: "Mind is the Buddha, and the Buddha is all living beings. It is not less for being manifest in ordinary beings, nor is it greater for being manifest in the Buddhas." This is Huang Po's way of saying that all is one, and whether it's ordinary or extraordinary, it's all an equal expression of spirit. It all has its ultimate value, ultimate goodness, and ultimate nobility. It doesn't matter if it's known or unknown. It doesn't matter if it's exalted or small, high or low. When we see with our eyes wide open, we see that everything intrinsically is an expression of divine reality and is filled with ultimate worth and value.

BEYOND THE WHEEL OF DUALITY

One of the things I've always appreciated about the story of Jesus is that he's one of the few figures in all of religious history who claimed to be both human and divine. Here he was, supposedly the son of God, and yet the son of God has very human moments. He has times when he's in distress, and even though he's in distress, he still has a gateway open to something that transcends what he's experiencing. Jesus wasn't somebody who was trying to transcend the human experience and get away from it. His vision was vast and immense. He saw that there was no ultimate difference between the human and the divine. As he said, "The kingdom of Heaven is spread upon the earth, and men don't see it."

In many forms of spirituality, the kingdom of Heaven, or freedom, or nirvana, is an escape from the world of duality. It's seen as an escape from the ups and downs and the turmoil of human existence. But what I have always found beautiful about the story of Jesus is that he didn't make this kind of distinction. To him, the world itself was the kingdom of Heaven, and what was beyond this world was the kingdom of Heaven, For Jesus, *everything* was an expression of the divine.

Jesus's life was a visceral example of living this kind of vision. He was very engaged in life, and he knew that to be engaged in life is to open "to the slings and arrows of outrageous fortune," as Shakespeare said, to open us to the way life really is: sometimes up, sometimes down. It is possible for our consciousness to be rooted in something beyond the world, in a vast mystery that the mind can never understand, but only experience. It's really just a matter of letting go of this relative point of view, letting go of our judgments, ideas, and beliefs. It's not that we need to get rid of these, but simply to see that they're actually relative, and they don't hold any ultimate reality. It is then that we can gain access to a whole new and other dimension of consciousness—a dimension of stillness and peace, a dimension of pure, vast spirit.

To realize that dimension as what we actually are, this deeper sense of ourselves, is extraordinarily liberating and incredibly freeing. And yet, that's not the end of our spiritual awakening. In the end, we'll have to let go of even that—not push it away, though, any more than we'd push away the human experience. Both the world of form and the formless nothingness are on the wheel of duality, but what lies beyond? Do we have the courage to let go of both Heaven and Hell, to let go of our attachment to not only this life on earth and our humanness, but also to let go of our attachment to the spiritual? Can we actually let go of the spiritual goodies, the great peace and freedom of nothingness, the great stillness of being pure spirit? Can we find a way to not grasp onto these, also?

Because if we hold onto the spiritual reality, we're going to have the dilemma that many spiritual seekers encounter, where they have a taste of Heaven, of the formless dimension, and their minds grab onto it. Many people discover that they want to stay in the formless dimension, but they keep getting pulled back here, to earth, by their jobs and their families and their children and the necessities of acting and being here. Then they seek and they seek for ways to be here without really being here. I meet a lot of people who've heard this saying of Jesus, "I'm in the world, but not of it," and they'll say, "Oh, that's what I want! I want to be in the world, but not of it!" But really what they mean is, "I want to be barely in the world, but what I really want to be is to be lost in that formless dimension of pure consciousness." That becomes very problematic. For one, it's actually impossible. In the world of duality, there's always coming and going, there's always life and death, there's always this moment and that moment, so we can't actually hold onto anything in the end.

I often remind those who come to hear me speak, "Even though I talk a lot, and even though there may be a lot of things for you to see, ultimately, the whole of spirituality is a process of surrender, of letting go, to such an extent that, even when you get the greatest spiritual revelation, eventually you'll have to let go of that too." I don't mean throw it away, like a piece of trash, but I mean let go of your attachment to it. Even among the spiritual communities that I've encountered, very few people know how not to get attached to Heaven.

The great sage Ramana Maharshi spoke a very well-known verse which is related to this: "The world is illusion. *Brahman* alone is real. The world is Brahman." Brahman means "God, the divine." The first line of the verse, "The world is illusion," is the first step in our awakening. We have to see that what we think, what we believe, what we imagine ourselves to be, is an illusion. This whole creation in our mind is nothing but a construct. It's quite illusory. It's not actually real, at all. This allows us to realize that Brahman, the divine, alone is real, that this formless state of consciousness, that place of pure being, unborn, is the reality. That's the place from which the whole world springs. That's what the world of form has its roots in. It is easy to get stuck there, however. It is the last verse that is necessary to bring us home to the real transcendental vision: "The world is Brahman." The world itself is divine. Ramana is pointing us there to the truth of nonduality, to the truth of the fundamental oneness of form and formlessness.

ULTIMATE REALITY IS ALL-INCLUSIVE

What we're exploring here is a total collapse of all of our dualistic points of view. This is a bringing together, a true union of the entire spiritual vision. Remember, the goal isn't to become spirit *instead* of human, but spirit *as well* as human. The goal isn't to become the divine nobodyness instead of being somebody. In truth, it's about realizing that what you are is a divine nobodyness, or nothingness, as well as a somebodyness and a somethingness that has a definite life to live. To name what's beyond both of these opposites, to give a name to what is neither this nor that, high nor low, something nor nothing, is very difficult to do.

In actuality, there is no name for this. Some of the Christian mystics called it the "Godhead," and they said that the Godhead is the spring from which God came. No matter what word we give for that which is beyond all duality, it's important for us to realize in our own being and in our own consciousness that the ultimate reality is all inclusive. It inhabits all worlds, all points of view. It's that formless presence, and it's beyond that, too.

I read that one of the Sufi mystics called this presence "the dazzling darkness," and I really love the sense of this, the feel of it. The dazzling darkness is not something that can be described. Who could ever say what it is? Who could ever say what's beyond light and dark, what's beyond spirit and matter? This is really a mature spiritual vision, not a vision that enables us to escape from the world, but one that liberates us enough to participate in it, to exist day to day from a fierce and open heart, from a willingness to fully meet and experience each and every moment. When our consciousness is rooted in this ultimate mystery, in this dazzling dark, in the ultimate Godhead, then we're no longer confined to Heaven or Hell. We're no longer limited to being spirit or matter. In fact, finally we don't see any difference between the two.

When we see with our true eyes, all around us is the divine. We were chasing for happiness, the end of sorrow, peace, freedom, God, enlightenment, and when we finally come to the deepest vision of reality, what we realize is we never had to go anywhere; the divine is always present. When we look out the window, there's a tree, a garbage can, the grass, a flower, a human being. All of this is actually the face of God. Look in the mirror; that's what God looks like today. Look out the window; that's your true self. That's your true nature being manifest as this moment.

Very few people understand what true nonsepara-tion is, but this is the invitation that's offered to us in any moment: that who we are is everything and nothing, and far beyond them both. The Heaven we've been looking for is here now, that very place that we've been looking from. Of course the mind will say, "It can't be! What about all the pain and sorrow and suffering?" The dualistic mind deeply wants, and it deeply believes, that ultimate reality has to be something other than this, but of course, if it's all one, then it's all one, and it includes everything. It is not necessary that we continue to experience suffering, despair, and conflict. These things are merely the product of a state of confusion, of being identified with a very small piece of the mind.

So it's not necessarily a fact that life is destined to include suffering, strife, and sorrow, but neither is life made to be perfect and absolutely heavenly, because neither one of those are the truth. What's real is beyond them both. And when you begin to feel or even get a sense of what I'm pointing to here, you might start to get a whole different view of the life of this moment. But you don't need to run away from anything, because there's nowhere to go. Here is the only place there is. Here our consciousness opens, and our ideas of ourselves expand. Here is a wider vision, of our unborn, undying nature, of our essence and source as pure spirit. And here it opens even more, and goes beyond the greatest heaven we've ever experienced. It opens into the dazzling dark, into the greatest mystery of being, where the mind will always be bewildered.

THE GREAT HEARTBREAK

This may sound far off for some people, a place unattainable, a state made available only for the few, but I can assure you that it doesn't require you to change or to become different at all to know this firsthand. It only requires a willingness to stop. The more we stop and the more we let go, the more our consciousness naturally opens. The more we question our conclusions, the more the doorway opens for us to have a wider and wider vision. The deeper we see into the reality of things, the more our heart opens to include everything, because if we're really feeling into our deepest reality and truth, the heart isn't something that would want to escape from what is here and now; rather, our hearts are already embracing everything. We can allow our hearts to be big enough to be broken.

My teacher called this world "the great heartbreak." When we really begin to wake up to our true nature, we become more conscious of the suffering around us. We feel the people and the events of our lives more profoundly, not less profoundly. We become more present here and now. What we see is that, even though our vision may have expanded, even though we may have woken up not just to reality, but *as* reality, still we can't control anyone. Everything and everyone has their own life to live, and we can't just wipe away their suffering because our hearts are open. Although we would love to have everyone wake up and be happy, part of the heartbreak is accepting this moment, this world, just as it is.

Another one of my teachers said, "All true love sheds a tear. It's bittersweet," and I've found this to be more and more true. The more deeply I love, the more I taste the bitterness with the sweet. It's not a negative bitterness; it's a bitterness that makes the sweetness even more sweet. Life is beautiful not just because of beautiful mountaintop vistas and the pristine, clear environment of a high mountain lake. Life is also beautiful in each and every moment. There is nobility and beauty even when human beings are suffering. Our hearts do not want them to suffer; we want to save them, but the heartbreak is that we can't do that. The quality of our love, the openness of our heart, still does have a profound effect on the world and others in it. Our hearts just can't control it—nor would they ever want to.

But don't ever think that your presence here—your physical, material, individual presence—doesn't have a great impact on everyone around you, because it does. You can't ultimately control what's around you, but you do have a great impact. This is the gift we have to give to each other: this gift of oneness, of union, of a true open heart that comes when our mind opens. Yes, it will be heartbreaking, and when our hearts break, it will be asked to open even wider, so wide that there's nothing and nobody to hold onto the heartbreak. But the heartbreak also moves through the transparency of consciousness. If we're willing to open that wide, to where we're willing to not just transcend this world, but to inhabit it and embody it, then we become the answer for which we've always been looking. Then we become the peace that all beings are seeking.

Sometimes it is disturbing to realize that we've been holding onto a pocketful of dreams, but ultimately, it's liberating. We can let our hearts break; they are that big. Illusion never brings peace, never brings happiness. When we're done being disturbed by our own illusions, then we start to become astonished—astonished that we aren't just our illusions, that we're something so vast and unexplainable. We're not something that exists *within* Heaven or even in the great mystery of being, but we actually *are* the great mystery of being. One Zen master said, "The whole universe is my true personality." This is a very wonderful saying: "The whole universe is my true personality." If you want to see what you truly are, open the window, and everything you see is in fact the expression of your inner reality. Can you embrace all of it?

11

Falling into Grace

I WANT TO return to the topic of grace and how it relates to this journey of awakening and moving beyond suffering. Grace is a difficult thing to define, to pin down; it's often thought of as a rather positive moment or event. However, we've all had experiences of extreme difficulty where, when we look back, we see that these were times when we transformed the most, when we made the biggest leap in our personal evolution. In retrospect, we view these challenging times as necessary steps on the path. We see that these events were infused with grace; they were a gift, something that was given to us to help us wake up.

In essence, grace is anything that helps us truly open— our minds, our bodies, our emotions, our hearts. Sometimes grace is soft and beautiful. It appears as insight. It comes as a sudden understanding, or maybe just the blossoming of our hearts, the breaking open of our emotional bodies so that we can feel more deeply and connect with what is and with each other in a deeper way. Grace can also be quite fierce. There are times in life that are very, very trying. At the time, grace might be hard to recognize, but as we think back to these powerful times in our lives, we can start to see the great gift that was received.

I remember hearing a talk from a very famous Tibetan teacher, a man who had spent many years in a small, stone hut in the Himalayas. He was crippled, and so he couldn't use either one of his legs. He told a story of how a big boulder fell on his legs and broke them, and he spent many years in a stone hut, because there was really nothing that he could do. It was hard for someone with broken legs to get around much in the Himalayas. He told the story of being in this small hut, and he said, "To be locked in that small hut for so many years was the greatest thing that ever happened to me. It was a great grace, because if it wasn't for that, I would never have turned within, and I would never have found the freedom that revealed itself there. So I look back at the losing of my legs as one of the most profound and lucky events of my whole life." Normally, most of us wouldn't think that losing the use of our legs would be grace. We have certain ideas about how we want grace to appear. But grace is simply that which opens our hearts, that which has the capacity to come in and open our perceptions about life.

For me, grace appeared that day I became so completely frustrated after four years of ardent meditation to no end. As I mentioned earlier, my experience at that moment was, "That's it! I'll never, ever be able to break through! I'll never find out what enlightenment is!" That moment was extremely devastating. It was like everything within me became absolutely exhausted. I truly felt that I was defeated, and actually I was. Nothing in me wanted to go on. Nothing in me had any hope for the future. I remember sitting in my little meditation hut, and I felt absolutely crushed. I became convinced that this was the end of my whole spiritual life, and I remember thinking, "What am I going to do now? My spiritual life is over. I've failed." And as I sat there in that moment of utter and absolute defeat—a defeat that was so total that I didn't even feel sorry for myself—right in the middle of that moment, my heart just began to flower. It was like a golden love was being poured right into my being. It was as if I could hear everything, and it was just singing with this love.

I went out of the hut, and everything I looked at was an expression of this love, a manifestation of this love. The whole universe was nothing but this immense, infinite love, which I was being bathed in. It was then that I heard a voice—which was very odd to me, because in my spiritual life, I wasn't prone to visions or hearing voices. I didn't know where it came from, but it just said, "This is how I love you, and this is how you shall love all beings everywhere." When I heard this voice, I knew it was true. This inner voice had told me something that I'd known all along, but I could never make contact with. What I didn't know is that I'd been showered with this love my entire life, but that I was never completely open to it. This love also put down a challenge to me. It said, "This is how you shall love all things and all beings."

I remember thinking, "I have no idea how to do that! How could I possibly love like this?" This immensity of unconditioned love was just washing over me in waves, and I couldn't possibly even consider how I could love in that same way, and yet, somehow, I knew it was possible. Somehow, I knew that it would happen. I didn't know when and I didn't know where, but somehow, I knew.

This was a moment of grace. The entire experience was grace. The feeling of being absolutely defeated, having nowhere to go, feeling that there was no way out, feeling totally despondent with my spiritual search: it was *all* grace. Sometimes grace cuts through us like a knife. It was this defeat that opened me up—opened my body, opened my mind—and it was only through this experience of being defeated that I could finally be open to the immensity of this unconditioned love.

This wasn't the last time I would feel defeated, nor was it the last time that grace showed itself to me. Actually, as the years went on, my whole spiritual life became one defeat after another. But with each moment of defeat, at each moment where I felt I was up against a brick wall I didn't know how to get beyond, I was stopped more and more. And each time I was stopped, grace would reveal itself. As time went on, I realized that I didn't have to struggle so hard, I didn't have to fight with life or with myself in order to open to grace. But it took many, many defeats before I could open willingly and surrender to the grace that is always there.

THE POWER OF A TRUE PRAYER

I've said many times, "My spiritual path was the path of defeat. It was only through this crushing defeat that awakening was revealed." People hear me, and they chuckle, but most of all they don't really understand. Of course, most of us are all trying to avoid this kind of defeat—this deep cutting of grace—as if our lives depended on it. Nobody could actually *want* to be defeated in this way. We've all felt moments of feeling pushed down or oppressed, but the kind of defeat that I'm talking about is a true surrender, a true opening, where we know that we don't know where to go. In that sense, it's a true prayer, and a true prayer is a very powerful thing. I often tell people, "When you speak a true prayer, you'd better watch out, because you're going to get what you pray for." And what I mean by a "true prayer" is one which is spoken, or made, when you open yourself to the entire universe, from a place of not knowing and not expecting anything in particular.

The first time I ever said a true prayer was when I was sitting in a vast desert at a bus stop in California, in a long desert that stretches between two mountain ranges. I was contemplating my spiritual life, and I suddenly had the impulse to pray. At that time, praying wasn't something that I did very often, but somehow, I felt this impulse. I said to the universe, "Give me whatever is necessary for me to awaken. I don't care what it takes. I don't care if the rest of my life is one of ease, and I don't care if the rest of my life is hellish. Whatever's necessary, that's what I want. I'm inviting it. Give me whatever I need to awaken from this separation." When I said this prayer, it was like giving the keys of control back to the universe. When I uttered this prayer, it was very frightening. I remember then thinking, "What did I just do? What force might I have unleashed?"

It became clear that I had unleashed a great force. At that moment, I gave my illusion of control back to a higher intelligence, and sure enough, I did get everything I needed, in relatively short measure, to really open my consciousness. Some of it was beautiful, filled with ease and love and openness, and some of it was rather horrific—very difficult and trying. But in retrospect, I had to admit that I got everything for which I asked. I got exactly what I needed in order for my own consciousness to awaken from separation. So never underestimate the power of prayer and its ability to open us to grace.

When we tell God what we want God to do, or we tell the universe what we want it to do, we're not really opening ourselves up yet—we're still speaking from an egoic place. But when we confess our deepest heart's yearning and tell the divine that we're inviting it to give us anything we need to awaken, we very well might get it. To open ourselves to this grace, to this flow of truth, means that we have to step out of ourselves. We have to let go of the illusion that we are in control of our life. When we hand it over, we'll find ourselves falling into grace, falling into this clarity and openness and love, falling right into the grace of awakening from separation, where we realize our true spiritual essence: this beautiful, unknown, unborn presence which manifests as everything we see.

THE POWER OF AN OPEN HEART

It's very easy for any spiritual teaching to quickly become conceptual and abstract. I remember my teacher often saying, "It's so easy for all this to become just talk, just words." And yet words are important, and the way we communicate is also important. We should never forget that all words, including all spiritual teachings are, as they say in Zen, "a finger pointing to the moon." It's not just the moon we're moving toward—the happiness, peace, and greater vision that we hope will come to us as a result of engaging in a particular spiritual path—but we must see that this "moon," or our true heart's yearning, is in fact also present right here and right now.

My teacher used to say, "The *Dharma* is good in the beginning, good in the middle, and good in the end." The Dharma refers to truth or reality, starting from the fundamental ground, the human heart, our deepest sincerity and integrity. This is what we have to bring to any spiritual teaching or to any aspect of our lives. The most important element is what we bring to these teachings. What is our state of mind? Are we truly open and available? Do we genuinely want to transform? Do we really want to wake up, or do we merely wish to shift around our life of illusion?

One of the most significant moments in my life occurred during my first Zen retreat. On the third day of the five-day program, the retreat leader, Kwong Roshi, told a story. In the story, he recounted a time that he had recently spent in India. He was standing in the middle of a dirt road in a little village, and he was watching some kids play at the side of the road. He noticed that there was one child with a deformed face and that the other children were teasing him. The boy was an outcast. Kwong just watched this poor little boy, and he said, "You know, I just stood there, and I didn't know what to do, and so I just started to sob."

Even as he was recounting the story, sitting in this regal meditation posture, with his robes and beautiful Zen style, he was very openheartedly weeping. It was then that I really knew of the quality of his heart and also of his courage. Here was one of the greatest spiritual authorities in Zen openly sitting there and weeping, without contracting, without hiding his face, without shying away. He had been deeply touched by this little boy's pain, and he stood there on the road wondering, "What can I do for him?" After a moment or two, he decided to walk over toward the boy. As they did not speak with same language, Kwong grabbed his hand, and they stood there in the middle of the street together, hand in hand. Kwong then noticed an ice cream shop. He walked the boy over to the shop, and he reached into his pocket and gave the boy some coins. He indicated that he wanted the boy to buy ice cream for all the other children, as well as for himself. When the little boy indicated to all the others that he would buy them ice cream, he immediately became the hero, the center of attention. Instantly, the village children enfolded him in happiness, love, and acceptance. This little boy bought them all ice cream, and they were all smiling. For a moment, this little boy who had been outcast and sad was happy, and he was once again part of the group.

This was the only thing that Kwong knew to do at that moment. It was a small gesture, but it was an example of the power of an open heart and mind. Even when he didn't know what to do, somehow, intuitively, because his mind was open, he just walked up and took the little boy's hand in his own. To me, this is an example of enlightened action. This is an example of how the mind may not be able to figure out how to respond, but how the open and awakened heart can take the lead and offer something beautiful in the moment. This kind of sincerity, this kind of openness and love is, in some measure, where we all need to begin.

We have to start our relationship with any teaching with an open heart and an open mind, as open as we can possibly be, and realize that it's we—each of us, individually—who bring to any moment in life the most valuable element there is. And that's our willingness to be open, our willingness to question, our willingness to care and be loving.

As I often tell my students, the person you'll have the hardest time opening to and truly loving without reserve is yourself. Once you can do that, you can love the whole universe unconditionally. But it all starts with you. These teachings also start with you. You're the most vital aspect of them.

When you're open and sincere, even the smallest thing can change your whole world, can shift your entire perspective, and you can begin to step out of suffering. This doesn't mean that you'll escape the suffering and challenge of being in the world, but your heart will become big enough where you can embrace the world as it is, with all of its beauty and all of its sorrow. And somehow, through that process, you become someone who has something revolutionary to offer this world—a truly open mind, an open heart, and an open consciousness.

FALL INTO THE CENTER OF NOW

Grace is all around us, if we only have the eyes to see it. The good moments are grace, the difficult moments are grace, the confusing moments are grace. When we can begin to open enough to realize that there is grace in every situation, in each person we meet, no matter how easy or difficult we perceive them to be, our hearts will flower and we'll be able to express the peace and the love that each of us has within us.

We let go into this grace. It's something we fall into, like when we fall into the arms of another, or we put our head on the pillow to go to sleep. It's a willingness to relax, even in the midst of tension. It's a willingness to stop for just a moment, to breathe, to notice that there's something else going on other than the story our mind is telling us. In this moment of grace, we see that whatever might be there in our experience, from the most difficult emotional challenges to the most causeless joy, occurs within a vast space of peace, of stillness, of ultimate well-being.

If we can let go for just a moment, if we can relax, if we can fall into the center of now, we can encounter directly the freedom that we've all been seeking. It is right here, right now. It doesn't lie in the future. It's not going to come when life changes, when the circumstances of our day-to-day reality become different. Freedom is something that's right in the midst of this moment. When we begin to surrender our demand that life change, that life alter itself to suit our ideas, then everything opens. We begin to awaken from this dream of separateness and struggle, and we realize that the grace we were always seeking is actually right there at the center of our own existence. This is the heart of spiritual awakening: to realize that what we have always yearned for is the very thing, in our deepest source, that we have always been. Freedom is always available to us. In those very moments when we know we don't know, when we take the backward step, heart wide open, we fall into grace.

About the Author

ADYASHANTI (whose name means "primordial peace") dares all seekers of peace and freedom to take the possibility of liberation in this life seriously. He began teaching in 1996 at the request of his Zen teacher with whom he had been studying for fourteen years. Since then, many spiritual seekers have awakened to their true nature while spending time with Adyashanti.

The author of *Emptiness Dancing, The Impact of Awakening, True Meditation, The End of Your World,* and *My Secret Is Silence,* Adyashanti offers spontaneous and direct nondual teachings that have been compared to those of the early Zen masters and Advaita Vedanta sages. However, Adya says, "If you filter my words through any tradition or '-ism,' you will miss altogether what I am saying. The liberating truth is not static; it is alive. It cannot be put into concepts and be understood by the mind. The truth lies beyond all forms of conceptual fundamentalism. What you are is the beyond—awake and present, here and now already. I am simply helping you to realize that."

A native of northern California, Adyashanti lives with his wife, Annie (Mukti), and teaches extensively in the San Francisco Bay Area, offering *satsangs,* weekend intensives, and silent retreats. He also travels to teach in other areas of the United States and Canada. For more information, please visit adyashanti.org.